The Corporate Healthcare Handbook

The Corporate Healthcare Handbook

Consultant Editor:
Helen Kogan

THE INDUSTRIAL SOCIETY

KOGAN PAGE

First published 1997

Kogan Page Ltd
120 Pentonville Road
London N1 9JN
E-mail: kpinfo@kogan-page.co.uk

British Library Cataloguing in Publication Data

ISBN 0 7494 21541

Typeset by BookEns Ltd, Royston, Herts
Printed and bound in Great Britain by Clays Ltd, St Ives plc

Contents

Foreword

The economic health of the nation is vital to this country. Success enables us to improve people's standard of living and the services we provide, such as education and the country's infrastructure.

An important contributor to our success is good health and there is a close correlation between good management and good health.

The government's initiative called *Health of the Nation* has a very simple message: 'it pays to be healthy' – easy to say, less easy to achieve. Employers have both a considerable responsibility and a very great incentive to invest in achieving a healthy workforce – it should be part of the essential infrastructure required to ensure that Britain succeeds.

Every company needs by law policies to prevent accidents and that has helped dramatically to reduce the suffering and trauma caused by death or injury. We have to build on that success. Just as many accidents are preventable so are many diseases, which cause absenteeism. This is bad for the company and usually unwelcomed by staff.

It is a good investment to help staff to give up smoking and if there is a staff canteen to improve the quality of meals so that staff get the food they enjoy with healthy choices. Companies which listen to staff are more likely to be successful. People are different; some thrive under pressure, others collapse. Accommodating staff to jobs that suit them reduces stress and mental illness. The CBI has estimated that mental ill health costs businesses 91 million working days each year. Their survey showed that a third of all sick leave was related to the effects of stress, anxiety and depression. Providing or encouraging staff to take physical exercise can be enjoyable, encourage team building and is healthy. Small investments can bring big rewards.

People who are fit work better.

If staff have to travel abroad, HIV infection is a terrible threat. It is often embarrassing to talk about but this is a case of prevention being better than a terrible death. You owe it to staff to inform them.

The Department of Health recognises that smaller businesses employing less than 200 people may not have the inhouse expertise to advise and help their staff. You can get the help you need from the Workplace Health Advisory Team (WHAT). Call them on 0171 431 1932.

We need Britain to be competitive and you need a healthy workforce.

WHAT is in it for you!

Baroness Cumberlege
The Parliamentary Under Secretary of
State for Health (Lords)

Introduction

Helen Kogan

Contributors to this, the first edition of *The Corporate Healthcare Handbook*, were asked to put forward reasons why companies should take their employee health seriously. As a result, both financial and humanitarian arguments run throughout the book for not only does it make good business sense for a company to safeguard the health of its most valuable asset – its employees – but there are overwhelming ethical reasons why workers should not suffer ill effects from work. The contributions to this book balance the two in an overwhelming argument for sensitive and preventive policies. Furthermore, many companies are now looking to positively improve the health of employees through health promotion campaigns and examples are given as to how these have been implemented and the results of such programmes to date.

Section one looks at the case for corporate health. Nick Jones' chapter examines the business arguments for managing ill health in the workplace. **The Business Case for Occupational Health** looks at the costs of employee ill health to business. He describes how compliance with legislation and fines for failure to comply, litigation, sickness absence, ill health retirement and private health insurance all have an impact on a company's bottom-line. Acting to improve the health of staff is not a question of 'whether or not to act' he advises, but 'when'.

The insurance industry is taking an increasingly important role in workplace health and safety. Janette Weir describes the current concerns of the Association of British Insurers in **Employers' Liability: A Role in Workplace Health and Safety**. She explains how Employer's Liability premiums are calculated and looks at some of the problems in pricing occupational diseases that have arisen from exposure that has occurred several decades in the past. She argues the case for preventive corporate health programmes by pointing to the response of more and more insurance companies who are offering facilities to support loss prevention programmes and offering employers reduced premiums in return. She argues, 'Improved risk management within the workplace will become increasingly important, resulting in reductions in the frequency of claims (and therefore the total amount of compensation paid). In the longer term, early identification of possible new occupational diseases and timely remedial action will benefit not only the insurer, but society as a whole.'

The argument for statutory compliance is presented by Joanna Lunn. She looks at current duties and explains the nature of liability in **the Legal Case for Corporate Health**. The concepts of 'reasonably practicable' risk assessments and health surveillance are examined and she suggests that if employers are to meet their obligations they need to be conscious of the concept of health, advances in medicine and diagnosis and developments in the law.

Section two examines the practical application of corporate healthcare policies. Stuart Whitaker looks at the subject of medical assessments of fitness to work and advises on when it is appropriate to carry them out in his chapter **Fitness to Work**. He examines the issues surrounding pre-employment assessments and raises the question of whether or not they should be used in all circumstances. Writing a health and safety policy need not be a complex affair, suggests Stuart Blenard. The health and safety policy should provide a 'map' identifying who has control of what and where responsibilities lie. His chapter **Health and Safety Policy** looks at ways in which a lay person can easily draw up a policy that meets with statutory compliance and the needs of the organisation. **Risk Assessment** is considered by Pat McGuinness. He examines the concept and ways in which risk assessments can be carried out and practical advice is given by way of procedures and standardised forms. **Needs Assessment for Occupational Health** is examined by Kit Artus. How to judge what kind of services are required for employee health and the inclusion of occupational health into other business areas are considered. A needs assessment system is also advised with examples of basic steps to follow. Dr Nerys Williams examines employer's duties and benefits when employing and rehabilitating disabled employees in **Disability, Rehabilitation and Employment**.

Section three examines specific examples of occupational disease with a range of experts. The scene is set by the Health and Safety Executive's Trevor Benn in **The Scale of Work-related Ill Health**. He describes the extent of occupational ill health and reminds the reader that 2.2 million cases of work-related illness in England and Wales were reported in 1996. Professor Newman Taylor writes on

Occupational Asthma and advises that early recognition and removal from its cause provides a better outcome for both employee and the employer. **The Stress Factor** is described by Caroline Toll. A workplace problem that is increasingly identified, stress, she says, can be reduced by organisations taking responsibility and by recognising it as a health hazard like any other. Failure to do so might lead to loss of trust and motivation and increased absenteeism, she warns.

Musculoskeletal problems in the Workplace have also been recognised as an increasing problem. Geoffrey Laycock looks at the legal duties of employers to prevent the occurrence of RSI and associated problems and provides examples of how practical action can be taken to reduce its prevalence. Dr Joanna Wattie writes on **Prevention of Occupational Contact Dermatitis** and its occurrence in specific areas of employment. Providing a prevention policy is possible with awareness, motivation and a logical approach to implementing policy in a practical manner, she says. With an estimated cost to industry of £20 million through skin disorders it is advice well worth taking on board.

Finally, section four looks at the ways in which companies are hoping to improve their employees' wellbeing through health promotion policies. I have examined the arguments for and against 'wellness' programmes in **Workplace Health Promotion: Providing a Rationale**. Ethical and practical issues are examined and the experience of workplace wellness initiatives in the USA are described. The Health Education Authority provides **Health Promotion: Case Studies** drawn from its annual award established to promote health and wellbeing of employees. Case studies include those from **C&A: Smoking, TSB Case Study: Stress, Post Office Case Study: Healthy Eating, LDCC Case Study: Physical Activity** and **Nissan Motor Manufacturing Ltd Case Study: Men's Health**. Each of these case studies provides examples of how companies have implemented health promotion policies and provide current outcomes.

Employee health continues to be a sensitive subject with ethical, practical, legal and business issues to be considered. I hope that *The Corporate Healthcare Handbook* has covered the main arguments in this field and has, as a result, encouraged readers to consider preventive policies to safeguard both business concerns and the wellbeing of employees. The loss to UK business as a whole and to the individual concerned is too great to be ignored, and with the insight and examples of best practice provided by this publication I hope that the inspiration can be provided to put in practice the current HSE campaign slogan 'Good Health is Good Business'.

List of Contributors

Kit Artus is director and principal consultant of Artus Associates, an occupational health and safety management training consultancy. She is a founder member of the Association of Independent Specialist Advisors (AISA). Artus Associates provide a professional and cost effective service in the design and implementation of successful occupational health and safety strategies in the work place.

Trevor Benn is a statistician in the Health and Safety Executive's Epidemiology and Medical Statistics Unit, which is responsible for collecting and critically reviewing statistics of occupational ill health, and carrying out or commissioning research studies to quantify health risks to workers. His particular responsibilities include editing the health component of the annual publication *Health and Safety Statistics* and managing a long-term study of mortality in British workers exposed to asbestos.

Stuart Blenard has more than twenty-five years' practical experience in health and safety covering many industrial and commercial activities. He provides practical advice and training for a wide range of business from mining and off-shore petrochemical power stations to banking, financial institutions, construction and general lecturing.

The Health Education Authority (HEA), as the nation's leading health promotion agency, has been playing a crucial role in encouraging the development of health programmes in the workplace. The HEA's team, based at Canterbury, launched a new Health at Work Awards Scheme in 1995 setting a national benchmark for quality standards in workplace health promotion.

Nick Jones is managing director of Sedgwick Noble Lowndes Occupational Health. His experience extends across the occupational health field, especially in the control of health-related costs resulting from sickness or employers' liability insurance issues.

Helen Kogan, a former editor of *Occupational Health*, is a freelance journalist specialising in occupational health and human resource issues.

Geoffrey Laycock is principal consultant of The Otter Consultancy. The Otter Consultancy provides a full range of investigative and advisory services on safety, health and ergonomics issues.

Joanne Lunn is a senior law lecturer at Manchester Metropolitan University and is also a qualified solicitor. Her teaching and research interests lie in employment, with particular interest in health and safety and discrimination against the disabled. In addition to conference presentations she is a regular contributor to the *Occupational Health Review* and *Tolley's Office, Health and Safety Practice.*

Pat McGuinness heads The Industrial Society's Health and Safety at Work training and consultancy activity. He is a qualified H&S professional and has been involved with the subject since 1971. He has written numerous articles and is the author of The Industrial Society book *Risk Assessment, a practical guide.*

Professor Anthony Newman Taylor OBE FRCP FFOM has been a consultant physician at Royal Brompton Hospital since 1977 and is head of the department of occupational and environmental medicine at the National Heart & Lung Institute. His major research interests have been in the field of occupational and environmental lung disease, particularly asthma. He is chairman of the Industrial Injuries Advisory Council and a member of the Medical Research Council Committee on Toxic Hazards in the Environment and Workplace.

Caroline Toll has worked for many different organisations and is now a freelance management trainer with a special interest in the relationship between individuals and organisations. She is co-author of *The Stress Work Book – how individuals, teams and organisations can balance pressure and performance*. Her interest in the subject began when working for her MA in Manpower Studies at London University.

Dr Joanna M Wattie FFOM is an independent consultant in occupational medicine. She worked in the Employment Medical Advisory Service of the Health and Safety Executive for over 15 years and was senior employment medical adviser for the East Midlands area for seven years until her early retirement in 1995. She was also a founder member of the National Eczema Society and has contributed to their publications on occupational dermatitis.

Janet Weir is manager of political and economic research at the Association of British Insurers. The Association of British Insurers is a trade body representing around 440 insurance companies, which between them account for over 90 per cent of the business of UK insurance companies.

Stuart Whitaker is a research fellow at the University of Birmingham and honorary lecturer in health sciences at the University of Wolverhampton. He has undertaken projects with the World Health Organisation, the International Commission on Occupational Health and the National Institute for Occupational Safety and Health in China.

Dr Nerys Williams is a graduate of Manchester Medical School and is an accredited specialist in occupational medicine. She is the assistant chief examiner of the Faculty of Occupational Medicine of the Royal College of Physicians of London and is an honorary clinical lecturer in occupational health at the Institute of Occupational Health at the University of Birmingham. She also sits on the editorial board of the journal *Occupational Medicine.*

PART ONE

THE CASE FOR CORPORATE HEALTH

1

The Business Case for Occupational Health Services

Nick Jones
Sedgwick Noble Lowndes
Occupational Health Limited

Introduction

Ill health is expensive, to employer, employee and society as a whole, and with costs continuing to increase the state is steadily transferring more and more from the Social Security budget to the employer.

The business case for managing ill health should therefore be straightforward. However, the real impact of these costs on an individual organisation is often unclear, and without such information the extent to which they can be managed is difficult to establish.

Intervention produces many benefits, some of which are directly measurable and demonstrate cost savings. Others are indirect or 'soft', but remain the major motivation for many employers. The way in which health-related costs are increasing is resulting in many of these 'soft' benefits becoming more quantifiable, making the case for the provision of occupational health services much more straightforward.

'Hard' and 'soft' costs

Until recently most investment in occupational health was based on a belief that, as in other areas of health and safety expenditure, we were avoiding, or more often minimising, the potential future losses that may occur. The cost of an occupational health service is however a 'direct' cost, often budgeted for as an overhead. The business case for occupational health, at least in simple financial terms, relies on the comparison of the 'hard' cash cost of provision against this concept of future cost avoidance.

Many attempts have been made to quantify these 'soft' costs associated with a failure to avoid ill health, either to the employer or to the economy as a whole, and without exception these have resulted in estimates of total economy costs in the order of tens of billions of pounds per year. However, until recently the proportion carried by the employer was often quite low, in the order of 10 per cent or less.

Over the past three to four years there has been a dramatic change in the way in which many of these costs have either been transferred directly from the state to the employer, such as in the case of Statutory Sick Pay, or in increasing demands on employers' pension and disability insurance schemes to replace income lost due to the changes in the Invalidity Benefit scheme.

The same period has also seen continuing increases in the overall cost of ill health, resulting from a combination of increased awareness of health issues, the introduction of contingency fee based civil litigation, and continuing commercial pressure to improve individual productivity. The Health and Safety Executive (HSE) estimates the total cost of work-related ill health to be between £170 and £360 per employee per annum, averaged across all UK employees (Davies and Teasdale, 1994). However, this is only a small percentage of the total cost which, including non-work-related illness, increases the average cost to over £1000 per employee per annum.

Current trends forecast that costs will continue to rise, and the point at which a pro-active occupational health service can be justified on a simply commercial break-even basis will be reached by almost all organisations over the next five years.

However, in order to realise the benefits needed effectively to control costs the occupational health service, be it inhouse or contracted, must function as an integral part of the management process, operating with clear objectives focused on managing the health issues within the organisation, and with full senior management support.

What are the costs of employee ill health?

The biggest single problem is that many employers have few if any mechanisms in place with which to record and analyse the variety of costs that they incur resulting from ill health. Often any mechanisms that are in place, for example, sickness absence recording, are not fully complied with, resulting in inaccurate data on which managers feel they cannot rely.

Potential ill-health costs include:

• Legislation	Compliance costs. Fines for failure to comply.
• Litigation for damages	Employers' Liability insurance premiums and excesses. Legal costs, record discovery administration, etc.
• Sickness absence	Sick pay costs and administration. Cover staff and training costs. Lost productivity, etc.
• Ill health retirement	Increased pension fund contributions. Administration costs. Permanent health insurance premiums and excesses.
• Private health insurance	Increased premiums.

Legislation

Compliance with legislation is the most common reason given for providing occupational healthcare. In reality there are, at least within the UK, few statutory obligations other than in a limited number of specific sectors, and a failure to comply has historically incurred relatively low financial penalties. There is of course the associated negative publicity that could result, but the inevitable civil law suit for compensation by the affected employees or their dependants would probably be greater than any fine.

Litigation resulting from accidental injury or occupational ill health has been increasingly extended into general health issues, with claims being made on the basis of the employer having made an existing health condition worse. There would now appear to be no limit to the conditions for which compensation is being sought.

Figure 1.1 shows how the scope of employers' liability insurance has developed since its inception. This growth of claims for diseases, as opposed to injuries, has been the primary reason for the significant increases in employers' liability premiums over the past few years.

Sickness absence

Sickness absence is usually the largest single area of cost, especially now that Statutory Sick Pay is no longer recoverable from the state for all but the smallest companies. A simple but effective system for the accurate recording, classifying and analysis of sickness (as opposed to other leave of absence) is the most important first step both to quantify not only the cost of absence, but also to identify the potential for reduction.

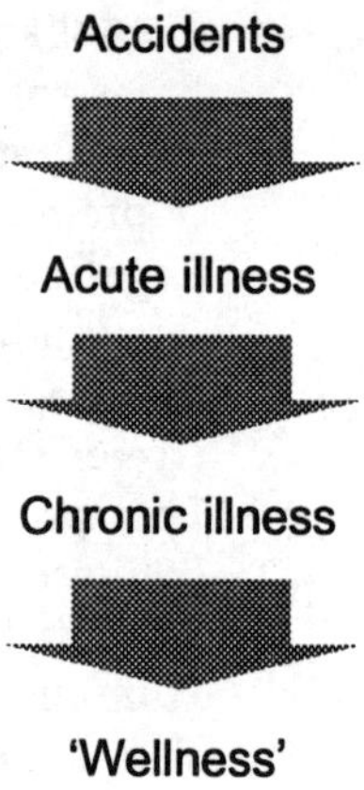

Figure 1.1 *The evolution of employers' liability insurance*

Invariably many absences are not recorded and what is set down often does not include an accurate description of the real reason for the absence. If cost information is included, this is normally limited to the direct salary or sick pay paid to the individual concerned, which ignores replacement staff costs, let alone 'lost opportunity' costs associated with reduced productivity. At a time when most organisations have 'right sized', the loss of a key employee can have a much increased impact compared with only a few years ago.

Pension and permanent health insurance schemes

Few companies with pension or disability insurance schemes in place will have failed to be affected by an increase in requests for early retirement due to ill health, which unlike employer's liability insurance, covers all aspects of general health. The cost of a successful claim will of course relate to the particular scheme, the number of years service and the employee's salary, but it is by no means uncommon for the total cost to the pension fund to exceed £200,000 and even higher figures are regularly found.

Many pension funds are no longer able to take on this order of cost without needing to recover some or all of it from the parent company, usually in the form of increased company contributions. In the case of permanent disability insurance schemes premiums are directly related to the claims made, and many employers have seen very large increases in premiums as a result.

Private health insurance

For those employers that provide private medical insurance for some or all of their staff, many will have seen costs increase at or above the general rate of inflation for the last few years, primarily as a result of medical cost inflation. Within the Healthcare Division of Sedgwick Noble Lowndes we have over the last two years seen an increase in claims for certain conditions, particularly musculoskeletal problems, which upon investigation have occurred either directly or indirectly as a result of the individual's occupation. The early return to work often facilitated by medical insurance is clearly a benefit, but rarely is the cost seen as a part of the overall cost of ill health within the company.

Lost productivity

The costs associated with reduced productivity are often the most difficult to specify, yet dependent on the type of operation it could be the biggest single area of cost. Reports from bodies such as the HSE, Confederation for British Industry (CBI) and the Industrial Society among others, argue that for most employers the productivity costs exceed direct salary costs by between five and ten fold. In the HSE report (Davies and Teasdale, 1994) on the costs of work-related ill health, even greater cost ratios were demonstrated, primarily due to production interruption. This would apply just as much to absence due to general illness as to work-related illness.

Accidents	*Illness*
• 500 killed per year • 15 million days lost	• 100,000 killed per year • 350 million days lost

Figure 1.2 *Lost employment resource*

For most organisations the total cost of lost time due to illness is at least ten times that lost due to accidents (see Figure 1.2). Yet how many employers commit the same amount of resources to health as they do to safety, let alone in proportion to their relative costs?

The total cost, including all of the above areas, will vary enormously from company to company. Factors such as location, age profile, occupational hazards and employee benefit package all influence the 'real' cost to that organisation. What should not be overlooked is that however expensive it is for the employer, the vast majority of those employees affected suffer much more financially.

In our experience, while there is a small number of 'professional

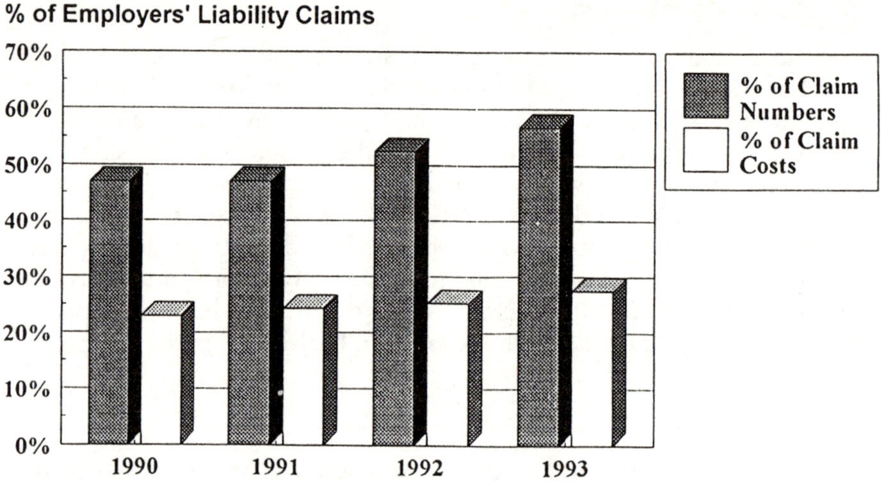

Figure 1.3 *Increase of occupational disease claims*
Source: Association of British Insurers

malingerers', the vast majority of employees with health problems would much rather return to full health and continue in employment. Yet without practical help and assistance many who could return to full employment are unable to do so.

Current trends in health-related costs

The current trends relating to both general health and the costs of failure to maintain health are unfortunately poor, with an increase in both the incidence of ill health and its associated costs.

Reported incidents of occupational diseases, with the exception of noise induced hearing loss, have all increased, no doubt as much a result of improved reporting as an actual increase in incidence. What is clear is that the largest increase is in claims for occupational disease (Figure 1.3).

The majority of these increases are for conditions such as lower back pain, asthma and stress. All conditions in which it is often not easy to differentiate between conditions caused by work, worsened by work, or simply reported at work. In today's litigious climate a claim is almost inevitable, and even if successfully defended the employer will still incur additional administration costs.

General health

Many of these conditions are directly linked to an individual's general

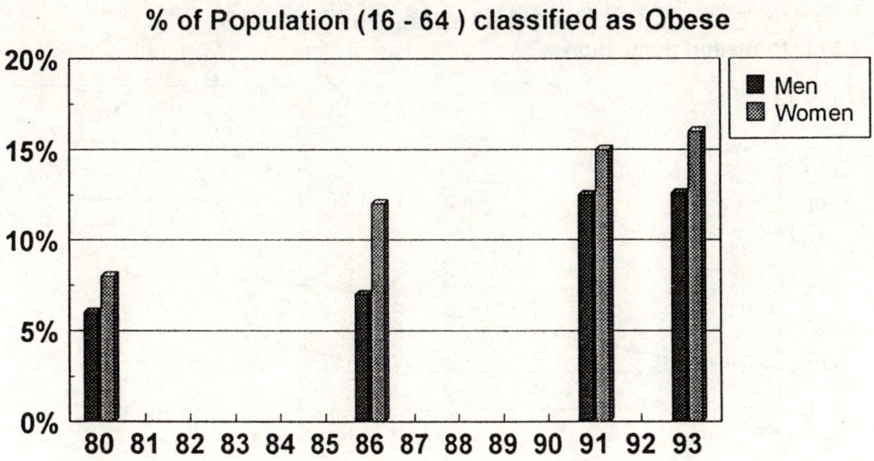

Figure 1.4 *Obesity increase*
Source: **National Audit Office – August 96**

health, and in particular their fitness, which recent surveys indicate is continuing to decline. The National Audit Office Report (1996) into progress on achieving Health of the Nation targets highlighted the continuing increase in obesity among men and particularly women (Figure 1.4).

But how does this affect employers? Up until recently few employers considered fitness as a part of the pre-employment assessment procedure, often to their cost. One of those that did was the British Army, which found that so many new recruits were failing basic training that they were forced to introduce a simple fitness test. This was to be completed prior to commencing basic training. The test consisted of two 'pull-ups', twenty sit-ups in a minute, and a mile and a half run in under eleven and a half minutes. In 1993, 40 per cent of applicants failed, and 42 per cent in 1994. With the failure rate increasing, the test was then revised to take out the stamina element. Where did the mainly young men who failed the test eventually find employment?

Back pain

Absence due to lower back pain was fully researched by the Clinical Standards Advisory Group (1994) which found that absence had more than doubled over the past five years, having previously only risen slowly (Figure 1.5). Some of the statistics have important implications for employers:

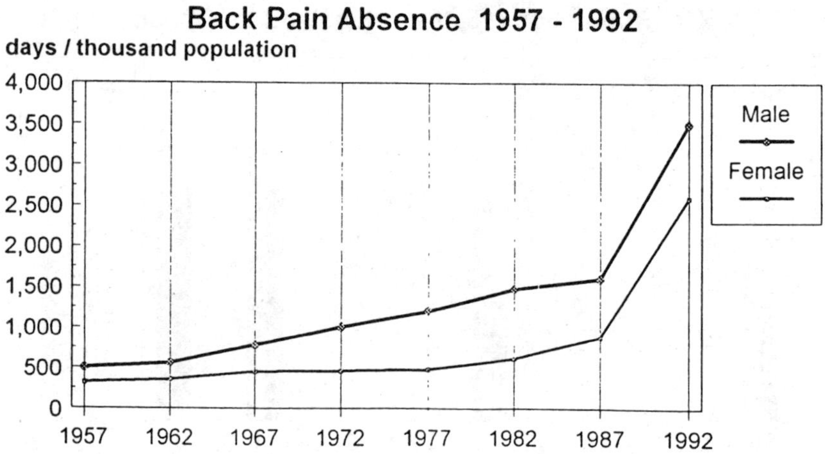

Figure 1.5 *Absence due to back pain*
Source: Clinical Standards Advisory Group 1994

- 37 per cent of all adults had back pain in the past year.
- One in seven adults will have back pain on any particular day.
- Only 6 per cent of those with back pain have so far taken time off work.

Exercise

Most employers would accept that a worker's strength and suppleness would reduce as they get beyond middle age. Almost all assume that an individual in their late teens or early twenties is 'fit', but this is often no longer the case. There is strong agreement within the medical profession that a general lack of exercise both while at school and work is responsible for the increases in obesity, reductions in fitness, and consequential increases in 'lifestyle' related diseases in middle age and after.

The government has reacted by including a requirement for a minimum of two hours exercise per week within the National Curriculum, but in 1994 only 25 per cent of schools managed to achieve this, leaving the UK with the lowest level of exercise at school in the EU (Figure 1.6).

At a time when the average level of physical fitness is declining among a large proportion of the workforce, the need continually to improve productivity has in almost all sectors placed increased demands on employees, compounding the problems encountered by fitness.

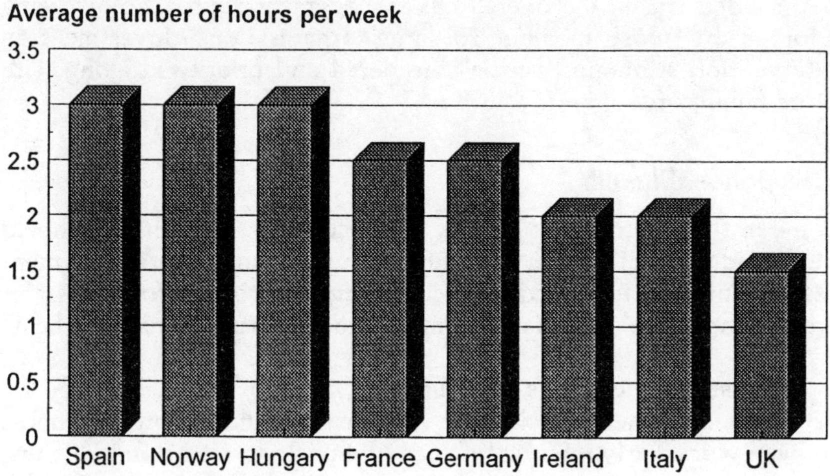

Figure 1.6 ***Physical education in secondary schools***
Source: **European Physical Education Associations**

Legal action

For those employees that develop a health problem, either directly or indirectly as a result of their employment, there is little doubt that the individual will consider taking legal action, especially now that the contingency fee system (no win–no fee) has been introduced into the UK. The Law Society objective last year was to increase civil claims for injury compensation by 33 per cent. At a time when awareness of the potential rewards available is at an all time high, the number and associated costs of claims against employers will continue to increase.

Intervention strategies

There is a belief shared by many employers that ill health is unavoidable, and that therefore there is little point in attempting to take any positive action. But with costs increasing there is a range of steps that can be taken to manage these costs more effectively, with improvements of only 10 per cent now being financially significant.

What is vital is that employers have a clear understanding of what their health costs are, and appreciate that many are interrelated. With this information clear objectives can be set, remedial actions piloted to quantify their benefit, and the whole issue managed as an integral part of the business process.

Investment in the tools that provide management with a detailed understanding of their health-related costs is therefore the essential first step in managing health costs. It also allows employee health to be included within the overall risk management approach now being adopted by most medium to large organisations. Investment in intervention strategies can be considered and prioritised along with more familiar risks.

Occupational health

Some of the services provided by the occupational health staff should be standard within all organisations, including pre-placement assessment, which is becoming increasingly important for fitness for work, employers' liability insurance and company pension scheme issues.

Sickness absence costs can almost always be reduced simply by acting sooner. There is no reason why cases should run on for months or even years. Early intervention can often help to return an individual to full fitness which may otherwise have ended up as an ill health retirement.

Rehabilitation has become a much more practical option over the past few years, with specialist clinics offering treatments with a very high probability of a return to full fitness, at a fixed cost equivalent to only a few weeks' sick pay.

These will help to respond to illness once it occurs, but the largest opportunity is in the area of avoidance of ill health in the first place. This approach is not common in the UK but is widely adopted in the USA where health costs are higher and directly charged to the employer.

Health screening

Health screening is widely provided in the UK, but often without obvious benefit. If provided on a voluntary basis experience shows that only the 'health aware' employees will take it up, and in effect you will be preaching to the converted. If the organisation is able to target those at risk, it should also consider how it can help and motivate those individuals with, for example, a need to increase fitness. Many approaches aimed to motivate have been used with varying degrees of success, but what is clear is that without follow-up support a one-off health screen is likely to have little benefit.

What is effective is the targeting of 'at risk' groups and working with them to improve their physical fitness, awareness of risks and best working practices, prior to their having actually suffered a problem. The most common area for this approach is in relation to lower back pain, which in many organisations can account for over a third of total absences, half of claims for private health insurance and employers' liability insurance, and a similar proportion of ill health retirement claims.

Health policy

There needs to be a clear policy in place before commencement of any health programme, so that everyone understands not just what will happen, but also what support will be provided to those employees who need it. Just as important, it will also need to set out what will happen to those who refuse to be helped, and become an increasing liability both to themselves and to the organisation.

Confidentiality needs to be treated practically and should be clearly detailed within the policy. Occupational practitioners are bound by professional codes of conduct to maintain employee confidentiality and agreed levels of exchange of information within the policy helps achieve management support when an employee needs time off for treatment.

Summary

Ultimately the objective has to be to encourage all employees, at whatever level, to take responsibility for their own health, and the employer will find it cost effective to give assistance in achieving this. Individuals who insist on ignoring such advice and assistance will become an increasing liability. There should be sufficient flexibility in the benefits schemes to give preferential incentives to those who have demonstrated their commitment to their own health, and indirectly the health of their company.

The point at which it becomes cost effective for a company to intervene in the health of its staff will vary with its age, sector, benefit structure and many other factors. What is clear is that almost all of the health-related costs incurred by employers are increasing. The issue is not one of whether or not to act, but when. Introducing systems to capture these costs is the first step towards being able to manage this increasingly important issue as a part of the normal business process.

BMI Healthservices

CHECKLIST

- ☑ **Is there a good system in place for measuring current health-related costs, and capable of demonstrating improvements?**
- ☑ **Have clear, measurable objectives been set for each of the healthcare initiatives?**
- ☑ **Is the cost of healthcare issues reflected in budgets and management reports?**
- ☑ **Is there senior management involvement in, and support for, the healthcare initiatives?**
- ☑ **Does initiative have a clear policy explaining the objectives and the responsibilities of the various parties, and is this fully documented and communicated?**
- ☑ **Is there understanding of, and funding for, any follow-up and support for employees needing help?**
- ☑ **Is the performance against agreed objectives monitored and reported?**
- ☑ **Is there a management process in place to review progress and set priorities for the next period?**

References

Association of British Insurers (1996) *Occupational Disease Enquiry*, Statistical bulletin, April, Association of British Insurers, (ISSN 1363–7231).

Clinical Standards Advisory Group (1994) *Epidemiology Review: The Epidemiology and Cost of Back Pain*, HMSO, London (ISBN 0 11 321887 7).

Davies and Teasdale (1994) *The Costs to the British Economy of Work Accidents and Work-related Ill Health*, HSE Books, Sudbury (ISBN 0 7176 0666 X).

Loss Prevention Council (1993) *Occupational Ill-health in Britain*, Report SHE 10, Loss Prevention Council, (ISBN 0 902167 65 0).

National Audit Office (1996) *Health of the Nation: A Progress Report*, HMSO, London.

The Costs of Accidents at Work (1993) HS(G)96, HMSO, London (ISBN 0 11 8863746).

2

Employers' Liability Insurance: A Role in Workplace Health and Safety?

Janette Weir
Association of British Insurers

Introduction

The risk of accident or injury at work is substantial. In the UK at present, there are currently 2 million people who are injured each year as a result of their work, resulting in over 20 million lost working days (Labour Force Survey, 1990). Around 200,000 people are currently in receipt of state compensation, with around 15,000 new awards being made each year; a further 130,000 claims for compensation are made against employers.

Insurance against the risk of work-related incidents is vital to the smooth running of the economy. Workers must be assured that they will be adequately protected against accidents and injuries arising out of the course of their employment. Otherwise they will withdraw from the labour market, or demand higher wages to cover their perception of the risk. Given that we live in a world where employees and employers do not have perfect information about the level of risk to which they are subjecting themselves in the workplace, perceptions are likely to be incorrect, leading to inefficiencies in the labour market.

From an employer's perspective, it is unlikely that all but the largest multinationals could afford to set aside sufficient reserves to fund large compensation awards. Even for these firms, it is likely that better use can be made of this money, for example, investing instead in capital projects which will expand the business for the future.

Insurance means that businesses can trade confident in the knowledge that if something does go wrong they will not suffer financially. If this confidence did not exist, many firms would choose not to trade in the first place. The insurance principle of pooling of risks means that the premium charged for individual firms will be lower than if each firm had to set aside reserves.

Insurance can be provided either by the state, through social insurance, or by the private insurance market. The UK provides protection through both mechanisms. This chapter examines the private insurance product, Employers' Liability.

Employers' Liability

People who have been in accidents at work, or have contracted a disease as a result of their job can also make a Personal Injury (PI) compensation claim against their employer. But to receive compensation, claimants must prove that their employer is legally liable, for example, due to negligence under health and safety legislation. This means that the system is adversarial in nature, with the onus of proof resting on the injured employee.

Successful PI claims against private sector firms are paid by the employer's compulsory insurance, Employers' Liability (EL). It is important to note that EL insurance protects the employer against the risk of being found legally liable to compensate an employee – it is not the employee who is protected by such insurance.

Claims against those exempt from having such insurance (central and local government, the police, the civil service, nationalised industries) are financed from general taxation.

Cover provided under EL policies typically indemnifies employers against legal liabilities for damages, including legal costs, resulting from claims for accidental death, bodily injury, illness or disease, arising from, and in the course of, employment.

Trends

The EL market in the UK is worth around £1 billion. Around 50 companies currently write EL insurance, accounting for 80 per cent of the market. The Lloyd's market supplies the remainder. The market is very concentrated, with the top five companies accounting for around two-thirds of all EL business.

Table 2.1 shows the proportion of the total value of EL claims attributable to different industries. Surprisingly the proportion of EL claims accounted for by distribution and retailing, and professional, clerical and other services increased considerably in the second period.

Table 2.1 *Sources of Employers' Liability claims*

Sector	*1984–8*	*1989–93*
Agriculture, forestry and fishing	3.8	2.2
Mines, quarries and related	3.1	3.5
Machinery manufacture and engineering	17.6	15.7
Textiles and clothing	6.7	3.5
Food, drink and tobacco	5.8	4.2
Other manufacturing	18.1	15.2
Construction	19.5	22.7
Distribution and retailing	9.4	13.0
Utilities and transport	4.3	5.6
Professional, clerical and other services	12.0	14.4

Source: ABI

Data from the ABI suggest that the average award is around £5,000. EL claims are generally settled within three to five years from date of notification.

Calculation of EL awards

Under common law, compensation is based on the principle of 'indemnification', which means restoring the injured party to the position he would have been in but for the incident.

Compensation under common law is calculated taking into account two factors. First, 'general damages' which compensate for non-pecuniary losses, such as pain and suffering and loss of amenity. Although no set rates exist, general levels are determined by reference to an informal scale which has evolved through judges' decisions on specific cases. This means that, in relation to each type of injury, compensation awarded today reflects the range of damages considered to be appropriate in the past. For example, payments for loss of both arms range from £85,000 to £95,000; payments for minor back injury awards are generally less than £5000.

Second, the award will include 'special damages' which will take account loss of earnings to date, and of future financial losses. Although each award reflects the particular circumstances of the individual, usual components account for:

- future loss of earnings;
- cost of medical treatment, including rehabilitation costs;
- costs of adapting living accommodation to accommodate the disability;

- more recently, payments in respect of loss of future pension rights have been taken into account. It is likely that this will extend to include spouse's loss of future pension rights, if pension splitting on divorce becomes more prolific.

Compensation is usually awarded as a lump sum, after which point the liability is discharged – although, if appropriate to the case, payments can be made periodically in the form of structured settlements. For example, if an employee has suffered a severe permanent injury and is awarded a large sum, it may be more suitable to his requirements for compensation to be awarded as an annuity payment rather than a lump sum, especially given annuity payments are free of income tax.

Provisional payment may be awarded by the courts if the prognosis is uncertain; in these circumstances liability for further compensation may be incurred.

Under the principle of indemnification, the amount of the award must be just sufficient to compensate the employee, over the period of his lifetime, for the injury. This means that, in theory, the award must be just enough so that on the day the employee dies, he has spent his last penny of compensation. Judges have traditionally calculated awards for future losses by applying a multiplier to the person's annual loss which, broadly speaking, is the sum of annual lost earnings and the annual cost of care (if any). This multiplier is based on age and expected investment returns, and is also adjusted to take account of labour market prospects. Rather than actuarially calculating each individual's multiplier, the courts generally follow precedent when choosing the appropriate rate, i.e. they look at similar awards in the past.

As economists and fund managers know, it is very difficult to determine what the appropriate rate of return should be, and then to forecast that rate into the future. Small changes in assumptions can lead to large variations in the amount of compensation awarded, particularly for younger people whose loss of earnings are likely to span many years. Accepted practices were to use assumed returns of 4 per cent to 5 per cent. However, the Ogden Tables, which are simply more actuarially based calculations of the multiplier, advocate using a rate of return of around 3 per cent. A lower rate of return means that the insurer must pay out a higher initial sum of money in order to compensate the employee. Some commentators have suggested that the lower rates could increase compensation claims, on average, by around 25 per cent. The effect will be exacerbated for younger employees. Increased awards may result in higher premiums for employers.

There is still some uncertainty in the judiciary over which rates should be used. Although the Law Commission endorsed the use of the Ogden Tables, recent decisions by the Court of Appeal have reaffirmed the conventional approach of using a discount rate of 4 to 5 per cent.

Pricing of El premiums

In theory, the premiums charged for EL policies should be based on actuarial assessments of the risk. Actuarial assessments are based on the number of claims made and the value of the awards paid. In a perfect world, each firm would be faced with a premium that exactly matched its own individual risk for the period covered. But in practice this is very difficult to achieve, due to a deficiency in information.

Insurance companies will often have different pricing strategies depending on the type of firm or industry. For example, many companies base their premiums for small firms on industry-wide data on levels of claims and awards. As Table 2.2 shows, this is the case for the majority of firms. In fact, the problem may be exacerbated as some insurers price on the basis of their own claims experience within that industry. So if, for example, one company had a particularly poor portfolio of risks in one industry, premiums quoted to firms in that industry would be high compared to competitors.

Employers are aware that rates may vary considerably from insurer to insurer. They rely on the advice of their brokers to ensure that each time they renew their insurance policy (i.e. on an annual basis), they are getting the best deal possible. Survey evidence has shown that, on average, employers move insurers every five years.

Where statistical data are inadequate, for example, where no previous claims experience on which to base calculations is available, pricing is based on the individual expertise of actuaries and

Table 2.2 *Distribution of firms*

Size of firm (number of employees)	*Number (000s)*	*Share of total businesses (%)*
0–4	3202	89
5–9	177	5
10–19	107	3
20–49	59	2
50–99	19	0.5
100–499	14	0.25
500+	3	0.25
Total	3581	100

Source: DTI

underwriters. Recent examples have included pricing risks for privatised industries such as British Coal and NHS hospital trusts.

Larger companies are likely to be rated on their own past claims experience, rather than the general claims history of the industry they are in. When rating companies, insurers will generally look at the past five years of claims. Some companies will also take into account factors such as:

- exposure to long tail risks, for example, a noisy workplace will be more prone to claims for industrial deafness;
- impact of large loss frequency and cost, for example, a factory employing hundreds of workers may be exposed to the risk of a large number of small claims, whereas a chemical plant may employ fewer workers but is more likely to experience claims for large awards;
- management health and safety programmes, for example, how new working practices can reduce the risk of exposure.

Pricing problems

The probability of an accident happening to someone working in a certain industry or occupation is fairly easy to estimate. For example, data are available from the Health and Safety Executive (HSE). Similarly, historic data on IIDB and insurers' own Employers' Liability awards provide a basis on which to calculate the likelihood of a claim occurring.

The risk of an accident occurring is a discrete occurrence – if one person in the firm has an accident it is unlikely that a large number of other workers will suffer the same experience at the same time. For example, if a man falls off a ladder one week it is unlikely that his colleague will fall off the same ladder the next week.

On the other hand, diseases are far more difficult to predict. In the first instance, it often takes many years for diseases to manifest. The workplaces of today contain unknown dangers for employees. To make matters worse by the time the dangers are identified it is too late to rectify the situation as the exposure has already occurred. This long latency period means that insurers are faced with a potential timebomb, as they are providing insurance now against diseases that have not yet materialised.

Furthermore, this problem is retrospective. New diseases appearing today, such as Vibration White Finger, may have arisen from exposure to workplace risks several decades ago. Crucial to insurers is therefore the 'date of knowledge'. This is the time at which employers should have been aware of the danger, and taken all precautions to prevent an employee from suffering harm. It is only after this date that liability arises. However, as this date is decided by the courts, it is often set some years before the date of the case. This leaves insurers with a liability stretching back a number of years, for which no premiums have been collected.

These difficulties are exacerbated because many employees are exposed to the same hazards at the same time. This means that, as a large number of people experience the onset of the disease at the same time, disease claims are generally bunched together.

These problems are well known to EL insurers. A report issued in 1994 by the City stockbroking firm Smith New Court (1994) drew attention to the fact that EL insurers have persistently under-reserved in respect of EL claims. In addition to the problems discussed above, some have argued that the highly competitive nature of the EL market at present, and the fact that EL insurers are not permitted by the Inland Revenue to put aside contingent funds for unquantifiable risks, are also contributing factors.

This has led to some insurers calling for a change in the way the business is written from an *occurrence* basis (where the insured can claim on the policy which was in force at the time the event leading to the liability took place) to a *claims made* basis (where the insured can only bring a claim during the period of the policy). There are many technical problems involved in such a change, and there is always the danger that once a severe occupational disease has been identified, the insurer may not wish to renew the cover. Furthermore, when employers go into liquidation, there will no longer be a policy in force to cover injured employees.

The role of insurers in workplace health and safety

It has been argued that the price of EL insurance should act as an incentive for employers to improve health and safety within the workplace. By improving exposure to workplace risk, employers would benefit from reduced premiums. Some have argued that taking this argument to its logical conclusion suggests that insurers would also have a role in monitoring health and safety provisions to ensure that the premium charged accurately reflected the level of risk in the workplace.

However, in practice, the role of insurance in improving health and safety depends on conditions in the market. At times when the insurance market is 'hard' (the supply of insurance is limited) the insurer is in a better position to insist on the insured improving health and safety conditions. When the market is 'soft' (as at present when there is a large number of players competing for business) the insurer has to take a more lenient attitude.

Moreover, EL insurers have generally priced policies, especially for smaller companies, in terms of historic data, sometimes on an industry wide level. This means the benefits to employers of improving conditions may take a long time to feed through into premiums, if at all. In addition, the cost of a risk assessment is often disproportionately high compared to the level of premium charged. Furthermore, the Employers' Liability Act forbids insurers to add certain technical exclusions to their policies. Therefore, policies often cannot exclude payments with respect to negligence or breach of regulation on the part of the employer or employee. Hence, it has been argued that employers may, therefore, take less notice of health and safety issues than if EL insurance did not exist. These factors mean that there have only been limited incentives for employers to implement often costly risk management programmes.

But this traditional attitude to loss prevention is changing. More and more insurance companies, and increasingly insurance brokers, are offering facilities to support loss prevention programmes. This support is sometimes provided as an additional free service to EL insurance, or to broker advice, and includes:

- regular health and safety audits;
- providing guidance and advice on the application of new guidelines;
- providing analyses of accident and claims data.

Some EL insurers share part of risk with employers through 'captive' insurance. This means an employer agrees to fund the first £x000 of compensation in any one year; the insurance policy will only come into effect when this limit has been exceeded. As employers have to set aside reserves to meet any liabilities up to this limit, it is in their interest to try to improve exposure. Employers benefit from this arrangement as they pay a lower premium, and a premium which reflects their current risk.

For insurers that offer this sort of package the gains are twofold: first they gain business in a highly competitive market; second they can offer the employer captive insurance management services – for which a fee will usually be charged. But not all insurers are in favour of captives. The disadvantages are that if the captive is inadequately funded, the insurer is still responsible for footing the whole of the bill.

However, it is important to remember that loss prevention programmes are only capable of limiting exposure to known hazards. But substantial strategic benefits can be gained by insurers if future industrial diseases can be predicted, or if high risk industries or occupations can be identified and targeted for remedial action at an early stage. The insurance industry therefore keeps abreast of developments in the medical world. It does this through several vehicles: by monitoring academic research, for example, reports in the *British Medical Journal*; by sponsoring medical research; and through research bodies such as the Loss Prevention Council.

The Loss Prevention Council (LPC), sponsored by the Association of British Insurers and Lloyd's, operates a long-term research programme to ensure that the insurance industry plays a full part in combating industrial disease. The LPC produces a series of publications devoted to topics in the general areas of safety, health and the environment. Recent reports have looked at such wide and diverse topics as asbestos use in buildings, vibration induced white finger and occupational cancer. Results from this research feed into the guidance and standards issues by the LPC to insurers, underwriters and brokers.

Latest developments

The EL market is currently in a state of flux. A number of important changes to the way EL insurance operates is currently taking place. These developments are briefly discussed below.

Review of Employers' Liability insurance

The Employers' Liability Act is currently under review by the Department of the Environment. Limits of liability were introduced by insurers for the first time in 1994 (when a £10m limit per occurrence was set). The main aim of the review is to ensure that employers are adequately insured within the constraints of what the insurance market is offering.

Woolf Report

A radical overhaul of the Civil Justice system, proposed by Lord Justice Woolf, will have far-reaching implications for the EL insurance market. Insurers in particular welcome his proposals concerning the development of protocols, based on a fair and equal exchange of information. These protocols will affect the insurance industry in two ways: first, by facilitating early disclosure of all relevant information; second, by encouraging the resolution of disputes before litigation becomes necessary. The Association of British Insurers, in conjunction with the Association of Personal Injury Lawyers, have been actively involved in the latter issue for some time.

Recoupment of NHS medical expenses

The reforms to the NHS in terms of stringent funding arrangements and the creation of hospital trusts have led to some discussion about whether medical expenses arising from industrial injuries should be paid for out of compensation, with the result that the ultimate burden would fall on EL insurance (whether through increased premiums or larger losses for EL insurers). At present, care is free at the point of use.

A precedent has already been set in current road traffic legislation, which permits certain costs arising as a result of a road traffic accident to be recouped from motor insurance.

Welfare state reforms

The future of the welfare state is under review. Fundamental questions about what kind of welfare state the UK should have – and can afford – are being asked by all parties. Industrial Injuries Disablement Benefit (IIDB) is one such area where both social and private insurance solution exist. Questions are being raised as to whether it is efficient to have two systems for compensation, and whether some or all of the social insurance scheme can be transferred to the private sector. An important part of this debate will centre on whether it is appropriate for the private insurance sector to take on all of the risks which the public sector wishes to transfer.

Compensation recovery

At present, the DSS deducts an amount equivalent to social insurance payments from compensation awards, where both payments have been made in respect of the same injury or disease. The only exception to this rule is where compensation awards are less than £2500, the 'small payments limit' (SPL). No distinction is made for payments due to pain and suffering and those due to loss of earnings.

New proposals, coming into effect in 1997, mean that the pain and suffering element of any award will be 'ring fenced'. This means it will be excluded when calculating whether benefit repayments are due. In addition, the SPL is likely to be abolished, and social security benefits will be deducted on a £1 for £1 basis from the remainder of the compensation award. It is difficult to say at this stage what the effect of these changes will be on compensation awards. Research commissioned by the ABI suggested that awards are likely to increase, with the ultimate cost being passed on to employers in the form of higher premiums.

Conclusion

The EL market is facing a very challenging period. Upward pressures on premiums are coming at a time when the highly competitive nature of the market is driving premiums downwards. This is resulting in large underwriting losses.

EL insurers are looking for ways to improve their underwriting position. Improved risk management within the workplace will become increasingly important. It is expected that this will result in reductions in the frequency of claims (and therefore the total amount of compensation paid). In the longer term, early identification of possible new occupational diseases and timely remedial action will benefit not only insurers, but society as a whole.

References

1 Labour Force Survey (1990) HSE supplement to the *1990 Labour Force Survey.*
2 Smith New Court (1994) *Employers' Liability Insurance – A Risky Business,* Smith New Court, London.

3

The Legal Case for Corporate Health

Joanne Lunn
Manchester Metropolitan University

Statutory duties

Modern health and safety law is to be found in The Health and Safety at Work Act 1974 (and the numerous regulations made under it, especially The Management of Health and Safety at Work Regulations 1992). These form the basis of corporate obligations although there are many other specific regulations.[1]

The Act itself ensued from the report of the Robens Committee.[2] However, more recently changes have emanated from European Directives which have placed emphasis on 'combating' risk and set new standards for health and safety practice. The focus has now shifted to risk assessments (e.g. risk of deafness, stress and skin complaints) and upon acting on these to eliminate and/or reduce the risks caused by the hazards.[3] (See Chapter 6) The source of the risks to be assessed are varied, for example, noise, violence and hazardous substances.[4] Although exposure to some risks may be general others are far more likely to be job related.

When carrying out risk assessment it is crucial that employers and those advising them appreciate the significance of the terms used in what is a growing science. Broadly speaking risk assessment means the acceptance of some risks and avoiding those which are too high. Risk assessment therefore usually involves the identification, comparison and prioritising of those risks that matter most. Risk management is the implementation of control measures. It is the application of a set of particular measures, for example, provision of appropriate equipment, heating and ventilation, to a set of risks intended to restrict and maintain the risks within a tolerable limit at a proportionate cost. Any residual risk will be that remaining after effective measures of risk reduction have been taken.

General duties

The principal duties are set out in Part I of the Health and Safety at Work Act 1974. It is important for companies to appreciate that they owe duties in respect of health and safety not only to employees but to all who may be affected by work activities, and that in the case of employees the duty also extends to welfare.

Employees

S.2 provides that:

> It shall be the duty of every employer to ensure, so far as reasonably practicable, the health, safety and welfare of all his employees.

Liability to others

As s.3(1) provides that:

> It shall be the duty of every employer to conduct his undertaking in such a way as to ensure, so far as is reasonably practicable, that persons not in his employment who may be affected thereby are not exposed to risks to their health and safety.

In effect a company may owe a duty both in the capacity of an employer and also as a person in control of premises.

The nature of liability

Lack of control

It is clear that liability for the conduct of the undertaking will extend to acts over which the company has no control and where it has delegated to an independent contractor. In R v Associated Octel [1974][5] the Court of Appeal rejected the submission that the words 'conducted his undertaking' in s.3(1) did not extend to acts of independent contractors over whom an employer had no control. Nor is the defence of proper delegation available.[6]

The court found that the only elements necessary for liability under the section are that the defendant is an employer, that he has conducted his undertaking to expose to a health and safety risk a person not employed by him who was affected by the undertaking.

The company had argued that s.3(1) merely 'criminalised' common law duties and that therefore control was a necessary element. The court took a wide approach giving purpose to the section. It was of the view that although at common law 'control' would be a necessary ingredient it was irrelevant in establishing liability under s.3(1). The practical effect is that for a company to be found liable under s.3 the prosecution does not have to show any definite level of control by the employer to establish liability. However, lack of control may become relevant as it may be a vital factor in establishing a defence of 'reasonable practicability'. The case follows an emerging pattern for the courts not to be unduly constrained by analogies with old common law rules.

Lack of actual danger

Nor will a company be able to argue (successfully) that there is no case to answer on the basis that there was only the possibility of exposure to danger and no actual danger. The Court of Appeal in R v The Board of Trustees of the Science Museum (appellants) 1994[7] have ruled that the possibility is sufficient it is not necessary for there to be actual risk to health for liability under s.3(1). It considered that the ordinary meaning of the word 'risks' conveys the idea of possibility of danger and that there is nothing in the language of s.3 or the context of the act which supports a narrowing down of the ordinary meaning.

Reasonably practicable

Companies may legitimately limit the extent of their liability by proving that it was not reasonably practicable to do more than was in fact done.[8]

This concept narrows the scope of the obligation as the company is not liable to do everything that is physically possible. A balance has to be made between the risk involved and the cost, time and effort in averting the risk. If the risk is insignificant compared to the measures to prevent it then the company will have discharged its duty if it takes no further action. On the other hand if the risk is significant this may tip the scales in favour of preventative measures, for example, protective equipment. Companies must make this risk assessment prior to the event. Hindsight plays no part in the assessment of what is reasonably practicable.

Relevant facts will be the size of the organisation, nature and gravity of the risk, the competence and experience of the workers and the nature of the precautions to be taken. Furthermore, companies will not be able to avoid liability by seeking to rely on the advice of experts as this is not a relevant criterion.[9]

The concept of reasonably practicable is in direct contrast to the new European Directives which shift emphasis to strict liability which imposes liability even where the company is 'ignorant of one or more of the facts which rendered [its] conduct criminal and even though [its] ignorance is not attributable to any fault or negligence on [its] part'. Many of the regulations are drafted to specify that the obligation **must** be done to a 'suitable and sufficient' level. Where the drafting expressly states that it must be done to that level, this creates a higher duty than the concept of reasonably practicable where the measures may not be met. In effect the new regulations create strict liability. In such circumstances the measures must be provided whereas with the concept of 'reasonably practicably' it is possible to argue that there is no need to meet the standard because it is not reasonably practicable.

Furthermore, it is well established[10] that companies cannot delegate otherwise liability could simply be defeated by delegating to an independent contractor. Companies cannot defend prosecutions under s.3(1) by arguing that the section should be construed as if the words 'through senior management ' were inserted immediately after the word 'employer'. The Court of Appeal, in R v British Steel 1995,[11] have stated that this would have the effect of driving a juggernaut through the Act. This was so even though the evidence might have suggested from the facts that delegation should be allowed as British Steel had 40 plants, 50,000 employees and 2900 employees at the level of purported delegation,[12] the law does not allow such a defence.

The court refused to apply dicta in Tesco Supermarket Ltd v Nattrass,[13] in which it held that the acts or omissions of shop managers were not acts of the company itself. It came to this decision as the latter case was based on the Trade Description Act 1968 which contains a specific defence that the company has exercised all due diligence.

In contrast The Health and Safety at Work Act 1974 does not contain a due diligence defence. The court also considered that health and safety requires more stringent protection than consumer protection. The case therefore reflects a policy approach attributing importance to health and safety protection in view of the spectrum of risks contemplated. It is therefore not open to companies to argue that the breach of duty was due to the act or omission of a manager.[14]

Nor may companies submit evidence regarding their finances when contesting an improvement notice.[15] The attitude of Industrial Tribunals is that it is inappropriate for them to consider the financial implications and that as a matter of policy it would be wrong to allow companies to ignore their statutory obligations and thus give them an unfair business advantage over competitors.[16] However, improvement notices must be confined to what can legally be required, that is there must be a specific breach of duty under the Act or regulations.[17]

Moreover technical defects will be modified rather than be used as the basis of cancellation.

Furthermore the burden of proof when seeking to appeal against a notice reflects the burden in related criminal proceedings. That is, the inspector need only prove the case on the balance of probabilities as the courts consider that it would be absurd if the burden was different.[18]

Corporate compliance

Companies need to consider the nature of their statutory duties and any limitations on these obligations in the form of defence. In order for companies to comply with the law and to promote corporate safety they need to focus on establishing sound health and safety policies and consider effective communication with their workforce through appropriate consultation.

Health and safety policies

Employers are under a duty to produce written health and safety policies.[19] In effect this forms part of a statutory duty and as such is enforceable. The duty is intended to promote health and safety and its effectiveness depends on corporate policies having appropriate content. (See Chapter 5).

Consultation

Another important aspect of effective health and safety practice is appropriate consultation. The Health and Safety at Work Act 1974 endeavoured to include workers through involvement with recognised trade unions. Prior to October 1996 only safety representatives appointed by recognised trade unions needed to be consulted, this provision has now been extended at the behest of Europe. The Council of the European Communities considers that workers must be in a position to reduce or eliminate risks, by means of 'balanced participation' and that safety and health at work must be developed between employers and workers. It therefore proposed that consultation requirements be extended to employees who are not trade union members of a group covered and this has now been implemented in The Health & Safety (Consultation with Employees) Regulations 1996. The employer can choose to consult non-trade union employees either directly or through elected representatives. Employers must give employees and their representatives enough information to allow them to take a full and effective part in the consultation.[20]

Employers will also have to comply with The Safety Representatives and Safety Committees Regulations 1977 if any of their employees are represented by a trade union safety representative.

Additionally under the new regulations employers are required to consult on the introduction of new measures in the workplace affecting health and safety of employees; arrangements for appointing persons to assist the employer in the implementation of health and safety law and evacuation of premises in the event of an emergency; information to be provided to employees; training for employees: and the consequences of introducing new technology into the workplace.

Risk assessments

Since 1978 health and safety has been part of the European Commission's Action Programmes. Member states were required to establish primary legislation to create a 'framework' for secondary legislation. The framework was implemented in the UK by the Management of Health and Safety at Work Regulations 1992. This established that employers should carry out risk assessment, which should be formally recorded[21] and monitored (See Chapter 6). These regulations require companies to identify the hazards that exist, assess the risk arising from those hazards and to establish effective control and monitoring systems. Risk can be defined as the chance of something adverse happening and risk estimates can be seen as a probability statement. Risks may vary from negligible, acceptable, tolerable to unacceptable.[22] Since 1992 risk assessment is now a fundamental requirement in all new health and safety legislation. Prior to 1992 it was an implied requirement of s.2 Health and Safety at Work Act 1974 to carry out risk assessment in order to provide a safe system of work.

The regulations go on expressly to provide that risk assessment should be carried out by a 'competent person' which raises the question as to who is a competent person. The regulations themselves define a person as being someone who has sufficient training experience to enable him to assist properly in the undertaking.[23] The Approved Code of Practice gives some guidance and accepts that who is competent may vary from organisation to organisation and that employers themselves may in limited circumstances carry out the function.[24]

Companies who use agencies to provide staff are under an obligation to tell the agency enough about the jobs so that the agency can provide appropriate training and health surveillance of its staff.[25]

Health surveillance

The 1992 regulations also place employers under an obligation to provide appropriate health surveillance and to protect employees' health in relation to identifiable occupational diseases such as asbestosis.[26] The keeping of individual health records is the minimum that a company may do to comply with health surveillance requirements once it has decided that surveillance is appropriate.[27] Companies should recognise that pre-employment health screening may have a role to play in health surveillance. It is well established that decisions to refuse employment on the basis of pre-employment health screening should only be taken on the basis of carefully defined criteria relating to the job in question. The Health and Safety Executive has stated that routine examination of all entering work is unnecessary. However it does recognise that it may be of value for furthering health and safety at work. In particular where the work is or may be hazardous unless certain medical criteria are met by those entering work.[28]

Access to medical records

In order to determine safety procedures the question of access to information to health of individuals may arise. It is paramount that any corporate procedures have due regard to the confidential nature of health and medical records[29] and the statutory restrictions regarding access to information. Occupational health practitioners will also be bound by their own professional and ethical codes. In the case of employed professionals companies should ensure that they have due regard to these matters otherwise in the event of dispute their requests for access to information contained in health records may be tantamount to an unreasonable order.

The future

In order to meet their obligations regarding health and safety companies will need to be conscious of the concept of health, advances in medicine and diagnosis and developments in the law.

Companies and their advisers therefore need to appreciate that health is not an absolute concept and that an individual's health may vary, for example, in cases where the illness may have remissions or be controlled by drugs. Companies need to have due regard to this when developing health and safety policies.

The possibilities of advances in occupational health such as new methods of screening, for example, genetic, and recognition of fresh occupational injuries/diseases[30] will also be of fundamental importance, as well as the evolving nature of legal concepts which is capable of recognising violence[31] to and harassment[32] of employees as a safety issue. Companies need to keep abreast of such changes and cannot be complacent. They need to review corporate practices to ensure that they meet their obligations and do not fall behind what becomes accepted as best practice.

Notes and references

1 There are many specific regulations for example:
The Construction (Design & Management) Regulations 1994 which apply in full to any project begun after 1 August 1995.
The Work-place (Health, Safety & Welfare) Regulations 1992 which came into full force on 1 January 1996 cover health and safety in the workplace.
The Control of Substances Hazardous to Health Regulations 1994 replaced the earlier 1988 regulations. They re-enact specific requirements regarding hazardous substances and have additional provisions in relation to exposure to biological agents. The Schedule prescribes control measures. The applicable one will be governed by the nature of the work, the probability of infection and the classification of the agent. It is vital that employers comply as exposure to hazardous substances is one of the greatest single risks. The 1994 regulations also revised maximum exposure limits expected to come into force in January 1997.
The Noise at Work Regulations 1989 these provide for noise assessment distinguishing between the noise being emitted on site and the noise experienced over the length of a normal working day. Compliance therefore involves a risk assessment based on levels of personal (noise) exposure, an action plan to reduce noise exposure where there is high risk either at source, buying low noise plant and equipment and providing ear protection.

2 1972 Cmd.5034.

3 See **Infra**.

4 There is no specific regulation requiring assessment of work-related violence although arguably it is an assessable risk under the Management of Health and Safety at Work Act 1992.

5 IRLR CA 540.

6 See **Infra**.

7 IRLR 25.

8 S.40 The Health and Safety at Work Act 1974.

9 Lockhart v Oliphant 1993 SLT 179.

10 R v Associated Octel 1994 IRLR 540.

11 IRLR 310.

12 Although the conviction was upheld the fine was £100 as the court considered the offence technical.
13 In that case the company was able to defend the case on the basis that the offence was due to the act of another person, namely the store manager, and that the company had taken all reasonable precautions and exercised all due diligence to avoid the commission of an offence.
14 Even when the defence is available in other areas it will not succeed if the directors of a limited company failed to exercise due diligence. In other words it is only available for failures of subordinate managers and similar employees where the company through its directors took all reasonable precautions, Pearce v Cullen (1952) 96 SOL Jo 132.
15 Notices may be issued by inspectors to enforce the statutory provisions rather than relying solely on prosecution.
16 T C Harrison (Newcastle-Under-Lyme) Ltd (appellants) v K Ramsey (HM Inspector) (respondent) [1976] IRLR 135.
17 For example, emergency stop controls on escalators reg. 19 of The Workplace (Health, Safety and Welfare) Regulations 1992.
18 Ibid.
19 S.2(3) Health and Safety at Work Act 1974.
20 The duty is not absolute and employers do not have to provide any information if:
- they are not aware of it;
- it would be against the interests of national security or unlawful;
- it is about an individual who has not given their permission;
- it would harm the business;
- the information has been acquired during legal proceedings.

21 Regulations 3(4) & 4(2) require risk assessments to be written.
22 **Negligible risks** are usually below one in a million per annum of a serious adverse consequence and where no thought is given to their likelihood in the conduct of normal life.

Acceptable risks are usually one in a million per annum of a serious adverse consequence and where no thought is given to their likelihood in the conduct of normal life.

Tolerable risks refers to the range of risk levels which is deliberately run on a regular basis for benefit.

Unacceptable risk is above the region of tolerable.

23 Regulation 6(5).
24 p. 222.
25 Management of Health and Safety at Work Regulations 1992, reg.10(1).
26 See the Approved Code of Practice para.30.
27 Ibid., para.32.

28 Health and Safety Executive, Pre-employment Health Screening, Guidance Note Medical Series 20, 1982.

29 The statutory provisions of The Access to Health Records 1990 may have particular significance in relation to employees' health records. It is arguable that such records are governed by the Act. Some occupational health professionals argue that their records are not caught on the basis that they do not have 'clinical care'. However, the definition of clinical care contained in section 11 of the Act is wide enough to cover examination. Furthermore health surveillance as defined by the Approved Code of Practice will fall within section 11.

30 For example, repetitive strain injury and stress. See: Walker v Northumberland County Council 199 IRLR 35.

31 The Health and Safety Executive has defined it as 'any incidence in which an employee is abused, threatened or assaulted by a member of the public in circumstances arising from his or her employment'. There is however an obligation to report such incidents under The Reporting of Injuries, Diseases and Dangerous Occurrences Regulations 1996. The approach of the Health and Safety Executive is to find out if there is a problem, record all incidents, classify them, search for preventative measures, decide what to do, put the measures into practice and check if they work.

32 For example, Gloucester County Council has now implemented a policy dealing with harassment at work and bullying.

PART TWO

CREATING CORPORATE HEALTH POLICY

4

Fitness to Work

Stuart Whitaker
University of Birmingham

Background

It has been suggested that the primary purpose of a medical assessment of fitness to work is to make sure that an individual is fit to perform the task involved effectively and without risk to his own or others' health and safety (Faculty of Occupational Medicine 1991).

There are a number of occasions when an assessment of an employee's fitness to work can be of real benefit to both employer and employee. Where there is any question that an employee's health or safety may be at risk from the job or when the employee may represent a risk to others because of their health, an assessment of their fitness to work by a competent, qualified occupational health professional is essential.

An assessment of fitness to work may be undertaken for different reasons prior to and during employment:

Pre-employment

- medical assessment as a statutory duty for specific jobs: for example, aeroplane pilots, merchant seamen, passenger vehicle drivers, commercial divers;
- health assessment prior to an offer of employment.

Post-employment

- pre-placement health assessment: for any post where new risks are likely to be encountered, for example, on promotion to a new position, job transfer or overseas posting;

- return to work: following sickness absence, industrial injury or as part of a rehabilitation programme;
- management referral: where there are concerns that an employee's performance, attendance or motivation at work may be affected by their health;
- self-referral: employees who suspect their health may be affected by their work or who feel that their health is impeding their ability to work should have the opportunity to seek advice from an occupational health professional;
- pre-retirement: the health of employees can be assessed prior to their retirement in order to offer advice about their capacity for work and non-work related activities in retirement.

An assessment of fitness to work is undertaken primarily to avoid placing people in jobs where they or other people may be placed at increased risk due to the health of the employee. It is not a means of screening out anyone with a medical condition or abnormality, as many people with medical conditions can and do perform perfectly well at work without representing any sort of increased risk to themselves or others. Sometimes quite simple modifications to the job or working practices are required to enable people with medical conditions to perform well and work in safety.

Pre-employment assessment

This section will focus upon one of the most common types of assessment of fitness to work – the pre-employment assessment. Employers frequently require job applicants to undergo pre-employment health assessment prior to a job offer, even when there is no statutory duty or specific legal requirement for them to do so.

Sometimes the aim and purpose of such assessments are not clearly defined or subject to any type of critical review. Some of the advantages, disadvantages and limitations of the pre-employment assessment are now discussed.

Aims and objectives of pre-employment assessment

Every organisation has a duty of care to protect the health and safety of its employees and others who may be affected by their actions. Many employers view the pre-employment assessment as a valuable tool in helping to fulfil part of this duty by taking reasonable steps to ensure that potential employees are fit to undertake the duties of the post prior to their employment.

Methods of assessment

In practice the pre-employment assessment can be undertaken in several ways:

- staged approach;
- nurse interview;
- medical examination.

Staged approach to assessment

The applicant completes a self-administered questionnaire which gathers information on their current health, medical history and any functional impairment. The questionnaire can then be screened by a qualified occupational health nurse who is familiar with the demands of the job. The nurse decides if the person is fit for the post. If a potential problem is identified from the questionnaire the applicant may be called for a health interview with the nurse and/or medical examination as appropriate.

Nurse interview as standard practice

An applicant is asked to complete a self-administered health questionnaire and to attend for a health interview with a qualified occupational health nurse as a standard practice. The nurse may perform a number of routine tests and clarify any issues from the questionnaire. If the nurse considers the applicant to be fit they will make the recommendation. If the applicant requires further investigations or assessment they will be referred to an occupational physician.

Medical examination

The applicant is asked to complete a questionnaire to record basic details on their health, medical history and functional ability. They may have a health interview with the nurse to administer tests and then undergo medical examination.

Current practice

Medical examination for all applicants as a method of pre-employment assessment has largely been abandoned in industry because it is considered to be an uneconomical and undesirable use of medical manpower (Health and Safety Executive 1982) and is not considered to be necessary for most jobs. Some employers still use medical examination for some job categories where there are specific hazards or where the appointment is to a key company position. However, employers should be cautious of introducing costly medical examinations at pre-employment assessment without first clearly identifying the need for medical assessment and defining how the process will be evaluated objectively.

The staged approach to pre-employment assessment, based upon the use of a self-completed questionnaire with onward referral to an occupational health nurse and/or occupational physician only when necessary has been widely adopted. The results achieved by this method in the NHS have been similar for those achieved through routine medical assessment (Whitaker and Aw, 1995). However, the staged approach is a less labour intensive, more cost-efficient means of undertaking the assessment which does not require all applicants having to attend for interview.

Results of assessment

The rules of medical confidentiality do not allow occupational health professionals to discuss the information supplied on health questionnaires or disclosed during health interviews, or to divulge information on applicants' medical conditions to non-medical personnel, unless the applicant has previously given their informed consent, usually in writing, for such disclosure to take place.

Breaching the rules of confidentiality can result in severe penalties for the occupational health professional up to and including removal from the professional register and their right to practice.

For an occupational health professional to function effectively the trust and confidence of employees must be maintained to such a degree that they feel comfortable discussing their health in an open and honest manner. Where there is fear that confidentiality may not be maintained employees may be reluctant to disclose relevant facts about their health and by so doing place themselves or others at risk.

Following assessment

The recommendations made by the occupational health professional on fitness to work are usually relayed to management in terms of the applicant being considered:

- fit;
- fit, with a specified restriction;
- unfit.

It is the employers' duty to ensure that they appoint competent professionals to undertake the assessment. This is usually achieved by ensuring that those undertaking the assessment are trained and qualified in the speciality of occupational health. This is especially important for nurses as many of them work in industry without specialist training or a recognised qualification. In many respects it is the nurse who undertakes the initial assessment of applicants and is relied upon to identify those with potential problems for onward referral. Where the nurse or physician has not received specialist training they may not be fully aware of the significance of their findings in making a judgement on fitness to work.

The appropriate qualifications for an occupational health nurse are RGN (Registered General Nurse) and OHNC, OHND (Occupational Health Nursing Certificate or Diploma) or evidence of having undertaken a specialist option in occupational health as part of a nursing degree course. For physicians the relevant qualifications are: AFOM, MFOM or FFOM (associate, member or fellow of the Faculty of Occupational Medicine). There is also a Diploma in Occupational Medicine which is designed to be an introduction to occupational medicine for the non-specialist.

Value of pre-employment assessment

Research studies of pre-employment assessment consistently demonstrate that very few applicants are considered to be unfit. In the largest study of pre-employment assessment conducted in the UK, which evaluated 9,139 pre-employment assessments in the NHS, 65 individuals (0.7 per cent) were rejected (Whitaker and Aw, 1995).

In a study of 101,754 applicants to the Dutch civil service, 0.6 per cent were rejected (De Kort, 1992). Other studies report similar findings: Schneider and McDonagh (1971) reported 100 per cent of 904 applicants fit; Lewy (1985) reported 99.5 per cent of 199 applicants fit; Harte (1974) reported 99 per cent of 764 applicants fit based upon a four-year study of those seen in his department.

This observation prompts three questions:

1. Why are the rejection rates so low?
2. Can the process really be of any benefit with such low rejection rates?
3. Can the process be cost effective?

The factors which may contribute to the low rejection rates at pre-employment assessment include:

- self-selection;
- safe working practices;
- limitations of the assessment process;
- subjective nature of assessment.

The influence of self-selection

The majority of individuals probably apply for jobs which they consider themselves capable of doing and do not knowingly apply for jobs which may damage their health. Their judgements will be based upon their knowledge and experience of similar jobs, information which is available to them on the proposed job and on their understanding of the relationship between their health and work.

Safe working practices

Where good standards of health and safety management exist the actual risks of the job may be so well controlled that for the majority of applicants, as long as these standards are maintained, there should be no significantly increased risk to the individual or others if they are employed.

Where individuals are subsequently injured or affected by work, this does not automatically indicate a failure of the pre-employment assessment to identify those at risk. The injury or illness may be directly related to a failure to maintain safe systems of work or even meet minimum legal standards for health and safety at the workplace.

Limitations of the assessment process

While it is relatively easy to weigh and measure someone or record their blood pressure or lung capacity and to identify a few cases which fall outside of normal values, the difficulty lies in predicting the significance of these findings in relation to employment. There are few objective tests which can be performed to assist in making the judgement about whether an applicant is fit for employment or not.

In the most obvious cases, where an applicant applies for a job for which they are clearly unsuitable on medical grounds, the recommendation can be made with confidence. However, in the majority of cases, including some of those judged fit, there is often a greater degree of uncertainty.

The assessment process is heavily dependent upon truthful answers being given by applicants and those with medical conditions may conceal relevant factors in order to secure employment. Social and financial pressures and the fear of unnecessary discrimination may encourage applicants to be conservative with the truth.

Subjective nature of assessment

The pre-employment assessment is a complex process requiring the occupational health professional to consider any condition which the applicant may have, in relation to the tasks they will be asked to perform, taking into consideration the employers' legal obligations not to discriminate unnecessarily, but also to protect the individual, work colleagues and others from harm.

Where a potential problem is identified the risk that an adverse event will occur and the nature or severity of that event need to be balanced against the consequences of rejection. Where the risks may be modified by changes to the working practices, job design or working environment to allow the applicant to work safely, these considerations raise issues of the practicalities and economics involved in making such changes. It is only when a judgement has been reached that a recommendation can be made.

Given the complex nature of the assessment and the fact that many of the decisions are based upon subjective views, rather than verifiable facts, it should not be surprising to find that there is often variation between occupational health professionals in their opinions on who is and who is not fit for work. In a study of five Dutch occupational physicians who were asked to review 180 pre-employment assessments it was found that agreement between the five was poor (De Kort 1992).

Can the process really be of any benefit?

Even with the recognised limitations of the assessment process and the probability that few applicants will be rejected, the process may still be of value if it prevents even those few applicants from significantly harming themselves or others in employment.

The economic costs and commercial consequences of employing someone who is a danger to the public or work colleagues because of their health could be enormous.

In addition, being able to demonstrate that due care has been taken in appointing employees and that a professional assessment of their fitness to work was undertaken prior to appointment may be of value in defending the employer against claims of negligence in the future.

Can it be cost efficient?

This is really dependent upon the most cost-efficient method of assessment being adopted. This may not mean adopting the most elaborate or expensive method of assessment. Where similar results can be obtained by a simpler process the employer would be acting reasonably in adopting the more cost-efficient approach.

In many respects when the limitations of pre-employment assessment are recognised and steps are then taken to ensure that other management strategies are in place to control workplace risks, the contribution of the pre-employment assessment can be seen in the context of the overall management strategy and can be designed in such a way as to be cost efficient.

Sickness absence or work performance

Employers sometimes view the pre-employment assessment as a means of screening out those who are likely to have high rates of sickness absence or poor work performance. However, the pre-employment assessment has been shown to be a poor predictor of sickness absence (Alexander *et al.*, 1975).

When all the factors which are known to influence sickness absence are taken into account, including the way people are managed at work, individual motivation, journey time, young children or second jobs, the relationship between ill health and high rates of absence becomes weak. Many employees with chronic medical conditions do not have high rates of sickness absence and yet others with no identifiable condition have above average rates of absence. Attendance at work may be more closely related to how employees are managed and motivated at work than to the results of a pre-employment assessment.

Having an effective attendance management system which actually deals with the causes of sickness absence as it occurs is more likely to reduce the overall rate of sickness absence in an organisation (Whitaker, 1997), rather than trying to screen out those with medical conditions at pre-employment assessment.

Similarly, the pre-employment assessment has been shown to be a poor predictor of work performance (Alexander *et al.*, 1977). Work performance is more likely to be influenced by good management, working practices, standards of equipment and levels of training or supervision on the job rather than by trying to improve performance through pre-employment assessment.

Summary

The pre-employment assessment, when applied for the purpose of identifying and assessing risks to health and safety, can be a useful activity when performed by competent, qualified occupational health professionals who are familiar with the demands of the job.

The process is likely to identify very few individuals who are unfit for employment, but these few cases may still represent a significant risk to the organisation, themselves and others.

The major benefit of pre-employment assessment is in matching the job to suit the individual and overcoming risks to the health and safety of employees for the benefit of the organisation, the individual and society as a whole.

References

Alexander, R W, Maida, A S, Walker, F J (1975) 'The validity of preemployment medical evaluations', *J. Occup. Med.*, 17(11): 687–92.

Alexander, R W, Brennan, J C, Maida, A S, Walker, R J (1977) 'The value of preplacement medical examination for nonhazardous light duty work', *J. Occup. Med.*, 19(20):107–12.

De Kort, W L, Uiterweer, H W P, van Dijk, F (1992) 'Agreement on medical fitness for a job', *Scand. J. Work Environ. Health*, 18:246–51.

Edwards, F C (1991) in F C Edwards and R I McCallum (eds) *Fitness for Work*, Oxford Medical Publications, p. 6.

Harte, J D (1974) 'Is pre-employment medical examination of value?', *Proceedings of the R.Soc. Med.*, 67:177–80.

Health and Safety Executive (1982) *Pre-employment Health Screening*, HSE Guidance note MS20, London.

Lewy, R (1985) 'Preplacement examination of temporary hospital workers', *J. Occup. Med.*, 27(2):122–4.

Schneider, R F, McDonagh, T J (1971) 'Experience data on university recruits hired without pre-employment examinations', *J. Occup. Med.*, 13(8):363–70.

Whitaker, S (1997) Focus on Sickness Absence. Working Well. *Health at Work in the NHS*. London. 4:6.

Whitaker, S, Aw, T C (1995) 'Audit of pre-employment assessments by occupational health departments in the National Health Service', *J. Occup. Med.*, 45(2):75–80.

5

Health and Safety Policy

Stuart Blenard
J & S Blenard Associates

Why have a health and safety policy?

To produce a health and safety policy statement just because 'it's the law' is doomed to result in a policy which is complex, unmanageable and full of words which do not necessarily reflect the practical aspects of protecting people and property at work. Likewise, some organisations employ legal experts to write the safety policy; the result is usually marvellous at protecting everybody except those at risk.

All workplaces are complex organisations, some more complex than others. The health and safety policy provides a 'map' through the complexity of an organisation by identifying who has control of what and who is responsible for what, when and where.

Health and safety provision within any organisation cannot just be left to 'common sense'. Likewise it cannot just be left to the safety officer or other person appointed to look after health and safety. All employees involved within the workplace have a responsibility for workplace safety, from the managing director or chief executive downwards.

Many organisations have wholeheartedly encompassed BS 5750 (ISO 9000) and produced excellent quality procedures and quality systems. Many are now tackling BS 7750, the Environmental Standard, again resulting in environmental policies and procedures covering everything from land contamination to the use of recycled products. Why? BS 5750 and BS 7750 are perceived to provide an edge on competitiveness and therefore, an investment is made by way of finance, resources and time, with the resultant policies and procedures being produced and followed.

A good, well-written health and safety policy will provide as great an edge on competitiveness by reducing the potential for loss and accident in the workplace, as well as covering many of the areas specified within the standards. The safety policy will establish a management system for health and safety which can be understood and followed by all.

With the introduction of recent legislation, namely the Management of Health and Safety at Work Regulations 1992, Workplace (health, safety and welfare) Regulations 1992 and associated 'six-pack regulations', plus the Construction (design and management) Regulations 1994, many clients are now requesting health and safety policies as proof of competence to provide a service or provide goods. A good, well written health and safety policy can now become a marketing tool.

Main benefits

- A health and safety policy is good management.
- A health and safety policy can contribute to the company by reducing loss.
- A health and safety policy provides a quality system.
- A health and safety policy shows your clients that you are committed to the highest standards of workplace health and safety, hence high workplace quality standards.
- A health and safety policy is a legal requirement where more than five are employed.
- The policy should be in plain words, not legal jargon.

Format for safety policy

Before starting to write the policy the format must be identified. The policy can either be a fully self-contained document, or can consist of the main document with the safety arrangements being produced as individual procedures. For a small organisation, the single document will probably suffice, while a larger, more complex organisation may choose separate procedures, as this provides for flexibility should an operation change or alter.

It must be remembered that the health and safety policy is a living document, not kept on a shelf to gather dust, but one which is in constant use. It must therefore be readable. It can be likened to a map providing directions on what to do when an incident occurs, or what action to take to ensure that effective safe process control is maintained. In deciding what format the policy should take, an early decision must be made as to the actual contents, what to include and what not to include. The basic contents should be:

- General Statement of policy from the managing director or chief executive;
- the organisation for putting the policy into place and ensuring that it is followed, i.e. who does what;
- the responsibilities of all levels of staff for ensuring compliance with the policy;
- the arrangements for carrying out the policy and how it is monitored.

CHECKLIST

- **A health and safety policy is a living document, i.e. may require frequent updating.**
- **The policy should be readable and understandable to all employees.**
- **The policy should be in a format which best meets the needs of the organisation.**

General statement

This is the commitment from the managing director or chief executive to ensure that high standards of health and safety within the workplace are met and maintained. It also contains the commitment for the health and safety of non-employees, whether contractors, visitors, or members of the public.

This statement must be positive and not a collection of words which has no forceful meaning. It should state that the responsibility and overall control of health and safety lies with the board of directors and ultimate responsibility lies with the managing director or chief executive.

It should further state that the board of directors will ensure that sufficient resources are available to ensure the implementation of the policy and maintenance of workplace health and safety. Likewise it should contain recognition by the directors of the importance of health and safety within the workplace. If the directors feel uncomfortable in making such commitments, perhaps they should not have accepted the position of a director, because there is an inescapable requirement to make this commitment.

CHECKLIST

- **The general statement must be a positive commitment from the board of directors.**
- **It must make a commitment to ensure that sufficient resources are available for its implementation.**
- **It should state where ultimate responsibility lies for health and safety.**

Organisation and responsibilities

Many health and safety policies start off with the words, 'The management ...', without defining who the management are. Such wording is not acceptable as it is sometimes difficult to define who the management are, especially when something has gone wrong.

The organisation for the carrying out of the policy must be defined in such a way that all people with a part to play must be identified either by name or job title. On many occasions, while tracing the true causation of an incident, I have encountered blame being passed from one individual to another with the ultimate get-out of 'it's the job of the safety officer'. All employees in every organisation have a duty towards their fellow workers with regard to health and safety. This duty cannot be shunted onto others.

A sad fact is that during seminars on this subject managers and others in many organisations are shocked to find that they can be held personally liable, could be fined or even spend time in jail.

Management is not only a case of selling to customers, meeting production targets, or keeping the accounts straight. It also involves a total approach which includes meeting an organisation's business objectives, but also of taking care of those under the manager's control, ensuring that they are not exposed to hazards at work, informing employees of the hazards and preventative methods, and checking that employees are competent to carry out their work in a safe manner.

The organisation for carrying out the policy must therefore be well defined. All those with a role to play (that is everyone) must be identified so everyone knows where they are. For example, the roles which should be defined are as follows:

- **Managing director or chief executive:** allocation of resources (finance, training, adequate levels of management, supervision, etc.), taking into account the health and safety aspects of any business decisions.
- **Purchasing manager:** should ensure that all substances purchased have been evaluated under the COSHH Regulations.

Should ensure that all contractors employed to carry out work either at or on behalf of the organisation are competent.

- **Human resource department manager:** should ensure that all employees, new and existing, are capable of doing their jobs in a safe manner and are medically fit to carry out the work.

  This also is applicable where an employee changes their job for the same employer, for example, where an employee is moved from a production line to a warehouse job, where the employee has a history of back problems.
- **Production manager:** should ensure that all production methods and production targets take into account the health and safety aspects of the job and corners will not be cut at the expense of health and safety.

  Should ensure that all production equipment is well maintained and that all employees are trained in the safe operation of the equipment.
- **Building services manager or facilities manager:** should ensure that the premises are safe and maintained in a safe manner at all times, that all maintenance is carried out by competent persons.
- **Safety officer:** is responsible for advising management of the requirements for meeting legislation; is responsible for liaising with the statutory authorities, i.e. fire authority, HSE, local authority environmental health departments, etc.

This list should be continued to cover all who have some part to play in ensuring health and safety.

The last item, but by no means the least important, is the role that employees are to play. Within each area identified, the responsibilities of each person should be identified with regard to health and safety.

An important but often overlooked detail is how health and safety issues, when identified, should be escalated, i.e. if a problem is identified on the shop floor, is it reported to the supervisor? What is the process when the supervisor cannot resolve the problem; is it escalated to the relevant manager? When in the process is the safety officer called in? These areas must be defined with clarity to avoid confusion and ensure speedy resolution of problems.

CHECKLIST

- **Use terms which identify individuals by name or job title, especially where the individual or department have a role to play in health and safety.**
- **Ensure that all managers know the roles they are to play, and why.**
- **Ensure that a traceable chain of command is established with regard to health and safety.**

Arrangements

The arrangements for health and safety are the actual processes which will be employed to ensure that standards are maintained and how they are audited. As stated previously, less complex organisations can include the arrangements or procedures within the main body of the policy. More complex or changing organisations may wish to create separate arrangements and procedures to allow changes to be made without republishing the whole policy.

The procedures are possibly one of the most important aspects of the health and safety policy. The policy cannot work unless a process is created to ensure that what should be done is done, how it should be done, who does it and when. This ties in with the previous section on responsibilities.

While different organisations will have differing needs as to what procedures must be produced, there are a few which are applicable to all companies:

- accident reporting;
- first aid;
- fire;
- use of substances;
- emergency action;
- conduct of risk assessments;
- manual handling risk assessments;
- visual display equipment assessments;
- maintenance;
- introduction of new technology;
- control of contractors;
- health and safety training;
- consultation with employees or their representatives.

Many others can be added, dependant upon activities and processes carried out within the organisation.

CHECKLIST

- **Identify those areas which the policy must cover.**
- **Look at the risks present within the workplace.**
- **Ensure that the arrangements reflect the responsibilities and organisational structure.**
- **Inform the individuals and departments of their role within the policy and seek their views; be prepared to enlighten them on their responsibilities.**

What should a procedure contain?

As stated previously, health and safety procedures can be either part of a quality system, or used as a quality system. The format I have found over many years, which works, is based upon the quality approach. Procedures can become long complicated documents which are never read due to their length or complexity. The approach which is successful is based upon simple, uncomplicated procedures which are backed up by working instructions giving more details and guidance for the department or individual which require it.

If, for example, a procedure is being written on accident reporting, the workforce only needs to know the essentials of how and what to report, they do not require the finer details of classifications, what notifications forms have to be completed and so on. This is the province of others. If it is decided to produce procedures and working instructions, produce them together to ensure that they fit together and are compatible. If the procedure states that form 1234 is sent to the HR department for inclusion in an employee's records, make sure that the working instructions state this fact and why.

CHECKLIST

- **Keep procedures simple and short.**
- **Ensure that the procedure and working instructions are compatible.**
- **Give reasons why certain actions have to be performed in the working instructions.**

Contents

Procedure number

In order to keep track of the procedures, it is better to have them numbered rather than just rely on titles. A catalogue of procedures can be produced which can easily be kept updated by number as against titles.

Issue number

As legislation changes or circumstances change within an organisation, there will be a need to re-issue the procedure to reflect such changes. One problem often met is where people are diligently following the wrong procedure or set of instructions in the belief they are the most recent issue. By using issue numbers and placing the procedures under document control, this problem can be eliminated. Such problems usually occur within large organisations and especially where the organisation has satellite offices.

Author

Procedures should always identify who wrote them. This is very important if a query is raised, or if somebody wishes to have changes made.

Approval

The health and safety policy starts with a statement of commitment from the managing director, or chief executive. However, this does not give carte blanche to the author to write into any procedures a commitment which the company must keep. By obtaining the approval of an executive, the procedure becomes part of the organisation's policies, along with quality and environmental matters. In addition, the authorisation also lends the procedure weight and authority.

Implementation date

Health and safety issues must be addressed before the fact, not as an afterthought. Most legislation has a period between being published and coming into effect. Procedures should be produced during this period and therefore require a date from when they are effective. Procedures produced to cover existing requirements should be made immediately effective.

Purpose

The purpose of the procedure must be defined in simple understandable terminology, for example:

- Reporting of accidents;
- Control of substances;
- Fire precautions, etc.

Scope

Not all the procedures produced will be applicable to all employees, areas or processes. The scope defines which groups have to take note of and follow the procedure.

Reference documents

Any documents which contain authoritative information should be listed. A procedure is a translation, into practical terms, of the requirements of legislation, etc. The source documentation should be listed so that anyone wishing to refer back to the source of the information can easily do so. Likewise should legislation change, if the reference documents are listed it becomes easier to identify which procedures must be reviewed. Reference documents can be other connected procedures, approved codes of practices or the company's own documentation.

Master document and working instructions location

It is surprising how many times organisations are not clear where master documents are kept – the master document being the latest issue which has the signature of the person giving authorisation and the date. This document must be kept in a central location under the control of a responsible person. If the procedure refers to working instructions as in the example, the master of these instructions will be kept with the procedure master. A traceable line of procedure formulation, process and control has now been established. Unless the documents are kept together, one or the other may be overlooked when updating. This not only could cause embarrassment, but could also be dangerous.

Procedure

The procedure must contain the actual process by which it is implemented and must take the user step by step through the process to produce the desired end result.

Responsibility

As with the main health and safety policy document, responsibilities of all who have to follow or act upon the procedure must be listed. This avoids confusion at a later date.

With the example, it could be the responsibility of the first aiders to report accidents and complete the reports. Likewise it could be the responsibility of the local manager or supervisor to investigate the accident.

Review and audit

No procedure is effective unless it is audited to ensure that it is still applicable, relevant or necessary for current circumstances. There is nothing which damages credibility quicker than having procedures in force which do not work. If such procedures do exist, the workforce soon starts to ignore not only those which are no longer applicable but also the ones which are applicable.

An important factor with any procedure is that some form of measurement can be made against it. Most procedures raised for health and safety purposes can contain a system of measurement. For our example, we can measure the number of accidents and compare them over a given period, identifying trends, etc which can enable corrective actions to be put into place before a serious accident occurs.

For the purposes of Control of Substances Hazardous to Health Regulations (COSHH), we can measure the number of substances evaluated against the number in use. Here again we have an audit process. A procedure is nothing but a piece of paper unless it is auditable and measurable where practicable.

CHECKLIST

- **Use a system for identifying the latest issue of the procedure.**
- **Place all procedures under some system of document control.**
- **Ensure that the author of the procedure is identified.**
- **Get top level approval for the procedure; it gives it credibility and enforcement.**
- **Ensure that the procedure is dated.**
- **Identify those who are covered by the procedure.**
- **List the main reference documents.**
- **Ensure that the procedure can be audited.**
- **Define who is responsible for the overall implementation of the procedure.**

Consultation

Under the Health and Safety (Consultation with Employees) Regulations 1996, employers must consult with employees on matters of health and safety where such matters have a significant effect upon the health and safety of employees.

The health and safety policy and subsequent procedures do have significant effect upon the employees' health and safety. Not only can the employee representatives make a significant contribution to the practical application of the procedure but they can also assist in its implementation.

Therefore consult with the workforce or their representatives on the policy and procedures. This will not only identify any gaps or problems but will enable you to spread the message as to the importance of the health and safety policy.

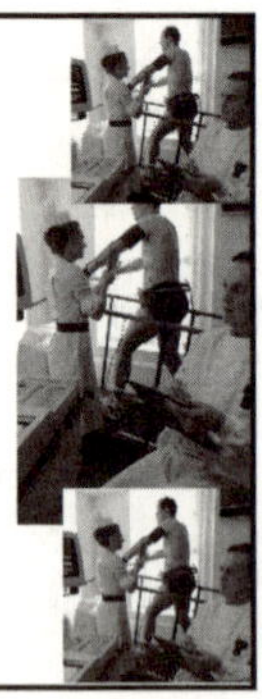

ACCIDENT REPORTING PROCEDURE

XYZ Company Limited

Procedure No: 000123 **Issue No:** 001

Author: AN Other, HR Manager **Approval:** IB Boss, Managing Director

Implementation Date: 10.10.96

1. Purpose

1.1 To define the action to be taken in the case of an accident occurring at work.

2. Scope

2.1 All employees, contractors, temporary staff, agency staff, visitors and members of the public, either on the premises of XYZ Company or working on behalf of the company.

3. Reference Documents

3.1 Health and Safety at Work etc. Act 1974.
Reporting of Accidents and Dangerous Occurrences Regulations 1995.
Health and Safety (First Aid) Regulations 1981.
Working Instructions, Accident Reporting, Reference 00123WI.

4. Master Document and Working Instructions location

4.1 Safety Department, Anytown Plant. Telephone: 0123 456 7897.

5. Procedure

- Put the actual process of how accidents are to be reported, to whom and what documentation must be completed.
- Define who is responsible for making an entry into the accident book, e.g. first aider, injured party, etc.
- Define how lost time accidents are to be recorded.

6. Responsibility

- Who is responsible for the completion of the accident book and internal reporting forms?
- Who is responsible for ensuring that all accidents are reported?
- Who is responsible for investigating the accident?
- What responsibilities has the employee?

7. Review and audit

- Periods set for the review of accident statistics.
- Periods for the review of the procedure due to legislation changing or new employees being introduced into the workplace.
- Audits to ensure the procedure is being followed, i.e. finding out if all employees are aware of the procedure and what to do in the case of an accident.
- Who is responsible for what actions and further notifications to HR department.

6

Risk Assessment

Pat McGuinness
The Industrial Society

Introduction

Every year in the UK between 400 and 500 people die in work-related accidents and 30 million working days are lost through injury or ill health. Studies have shown that there are about 1.6 million accidents at work each year in the UK. The appalling human cost of this is difficult to comprehend, unless you are unfortunate enough to have been involved as either victim, relative, colleague or manager. Both the financial implications for organisations and the country's economy are staggering. Health and Safety Executive (HSE) studies show that the cost of work accidents to employers could be as high as £9000 million per year, and the cost to the economy of work-related ill health is estimated as being between £10 billion and £15 billion per year.

When considering this background it can be readily understood why new and more specific legislation is being introduced. The new legislation is making explicit what was implicit in the Health and Safety at Work Act 1974. It is placing emphasis and focus on what needs to be done to raise the standard of our management of health and safety at work.

It is also interesting to note the consistent rise in fines for breaches of health and safety legislation. Organisations who break the law can expect to receive large fines together with huge legal costs. Individuals who are proven to have breached the law, are often prosecuted, including directors, managers, supervisors and employees. They are likely to receive personal fines, community service awards and, in severe cases, imprisonment.

Risk assessment is a proactive activity that helps organisations to avoid harming people and incurring losses, whether financial or in the form of service or activity that they provide. In reality a successful risk assessment programme will make the organisation more effective at what it does.

Background

The requirement to carry out risk assessments is driven by the three main reasons for managing health and safety at work:

- moral reasons;
- legal reasons;
- economic reasons.

Moral reasons

Not many people would wish to see illness, injury or death caused by the workplaces and work activities that they control. It is extremely upsetting for all concerned when a serious accident takes place. It is difficult to have to tell the relatives of the injured what has happened to their loved one. It is even more difficult to attend the funeral of someone who has been killed by the activities of the organisation. How do you face the bereaved family? What can you say?

Legal reasons

This is classed by some people as the CYA factor (cover your ...). There is no doubt that the law is being tightened up with more and more specific regulations. Most recently introduced regulations include a requirement to carry out risk assessments. This is not as novel as some people believe. The Health and Safety at Work Act 1974 carried a implicit requirement to assess risks; in fact you cannot fully comply with the act without doing so.

Fig 6.1 shows how the levels of duty overlap, starting with the Health and Safety at Work Act 1974, moving through the Management of Health and Safety at Work Regulations 1992 on to the most specific regulations, such as COSHH, DSE, etc.

Some of the specific regulations requiring risk assessments include:

- Manual Handling Operations Regulations 1992;
- (PPE) Personal Protective Equipment at Work Regulations 1992;
- (DSE) Display Screen Equipment Regulations 1992;
- Noise at Work Regulations 1989;
- (COSHH) Control of Substances Hazardous to Health Regulations 1994;
- Control of Asbestos at Work Regulations 1987;
- Control of Lead at Work Regulations 1980.

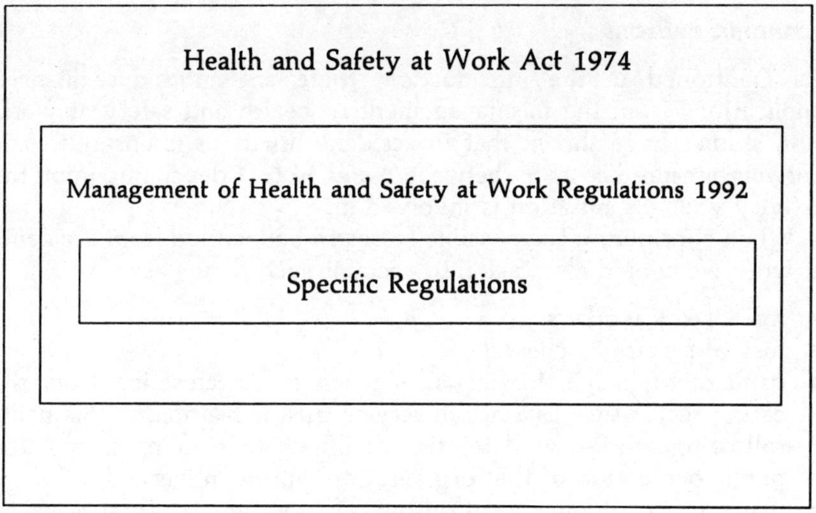

Figure 6.1 ***Overlap of levels of duty of regulations***

You should comply with the highest level of duty in any situation, usually the more specific regulations.

The Management of Health and Safety at Work Regulations 1992 include the following general duty:

> The carrying out of suitable and sufficient risk assessment of all risks to the health and safety of employees and non employees (in fact anyone), arising from the work activities and the identification of the necessary preventative and protective measures to prevent injury.

A risk assessment that is suitable and sufficient is defined in the ACOP (Approved Code Of Practice) to these regulations as follows:

- it should identify the significant risks arising out of work;
- it should enable the employer or self-employed person to identify and prioritise the measures that need to be taken to comply with the relevant statutory provisions;
- it should be appropriate to the nature of the work and such that it remains valid for a reasonable period of time.

The duty to assess risks under these regulations is general, to cover all eventualities arising at and from work. If a more specific regulation (i.e. COSHH, DSE, PPE or Manual Handling) applies to an activity or situation, it will not be necessary to repeat the existing risk assessment carried out for those regulations, providing:

- the assessment is still valid;
- the assessment is 'suitable and sufficient'.

Economic reasons

As mentioned in the introduction, there are enormous financial implications from the mismanagement of health and safety at work. HSE studies have shown that in accident situations, uninsured costs outweigh insured costs by between 8 and 36 to 1 depending upon the activity your organisation is involved in.

When considering the possible losses to be incurred from accidents at work we should also take into account such things as:

- loss of key workers;
- loss of service to clients;
- damage to image, for instance, when an organisation from the caring sector such as a health service trust is featured in the media following work-related injuries or illness to staff or clients, the public perception of that organisation will be influenced;
- damage to supplier relationship; if you are a Total Quality Organisation and you suffer accidents which are featured in the media, what is implied about your management control systems and how would this be interpreted by your major customers?

In general, risk assessment is only common sense. We would never cross a busy street without looking to see if it was safe to do so (an everyday example of risk assessment).

Methods of carrying out risk assessments

The various regulations do not define how risk assessments should be carried out; they only guide us as to what the outcome of risk assessment should be. This gives us the option of selecting a method that suits our organisation's particular needs.

Therefore there is no one method that will suit all organisations, it is recommended that a method that broadly fits what the organisation needs is taken and adapted to fit the specific situation. In this section we outline some popular and effective methods that are in use.

Some important definitions

Hazard – something with the **potential** to cause harm.

Risk – the likelihood of that potential to do harm being realised.

Risk assessment is a process of identifying the hazards in any work situation and making a competent judgement as to the likelihood of that hazard actually causing a risk of harm. Rating the severity of that risk and identifying measures to ensure that the risks are eliminated or, if that is not possible, adequately controlled so as to prevent harm.

Preventive and protective measures are those measures that have to be taken as a result of carrying out a risk assessment. Some are dependant on the specific legislation involved but HSE guidance is as follows:

- if possible avoid the risk altogether;
- combat risks at source;
- wherever possible adapt the work to the individual;
- take advantage of technological and technical progress;
- risk prevention measures need to form part of a coherent policy and approach;
- give a priority to those measures which protect the whole workplace and those who work there or visit it;
- workers need to understand what they need to do;
- the measures should be part of an approach that builds an active health and safety culture in the organisation.

The combating of risk at source is an important point to grasp. All too often we treat the symptom rather than the root cause. If we regularly find water on the floor, yes it is important to clean it up and prevent people slipping on it, but it is vital that we repair the faulty tap that is the real cause of the risk.

Some examples of risk assessment methods

The following are examples of methods currently being used by organisations:

- 5 steps to risk assessment;
- team-based risk assessment;
- computer-based risk assessment.

Five steps to risk assessment

This is a very easy-to-use system published by the HSE in Great Britain and the HSA in Northern Ireland. This well thought out, two-piece form (HSE Leaflet IND(G) 163L) consists of one sheet giving useful advice to guide the user through each of the five steps, and a second sheet with headings and prompts for the steps, with a column under each heading to record your findings.

The five steps to risk assessment process is:

1. Look for hazards.
2. Decide who might be harmed, and how.
3. Evaluate the risks arising from the hazards and decide whether existing precautions are adequate or more should be done.
4. Record your findings.

5. Review your assessment from time to time and revise it if necessary.

This system should be suitable for most organisations. Some people have commented that it is not sophisticated enough. However, it is our experience that simple effective systems get used, and deliver the required result.

Team-based risk assessment

This is another easy-to-use, form-based system that ensures that the risk assessment process is a team activity. The system was developed by The Industrial Society and is based on the logic that drives such initiatives as Quality Circles and Product Improvement Groups. It harnesses people's creative powers and gets them involved not just with designing safer working practices but more productive and economic outcomes.

The process of team-based risk assessment

The principle is to get the people close to the action involved, similar to product improvement groups. The team studies the method(s) being used to carry out an activity or the features of a work area. This is done by breaking the activity down into component parts (easily digestible chunks) and asking the following questions about each stage:

1. Are any hazards present?
2. Do those hazards represent a risk, and if so do we rate the risk as a low, medium or high?
3. Are we using the most appropriate method, equipment, material for what we are trying to achieve?
4. If we are, what controlling action(s) is/are necessary?
5. How are the controls to be implemented?
6. When?
7. Who is involved?
8. What monitoring is to be carried out, how often, and who is involved?

The team should be encouraged to estimate:

- the cost of any changes required;
- the likely benefits of proposed changes.

An example of how this works in practice is illustrated by a training example of sharpening a pencil with a penknife. The trainees assess this task as a team-based risk assessment, breaking it down into key stages. It is quickly ascertained that the wrong method is being used for the job and that a pencil sharpener would be better.

Making that simple change helps avoid potentially expensive and painful accidents, saves on raw materials (pencils, and possibly fingers!) and makes the job faster, requiring less skill and attention. The quality of the output is improved.

This is a simple example of an unsafe, incorrect method being used to achieve an end. But how many examples of this type are present in our workplaces? Figure 6.2 shows a typical team-based risk assessment form.

Computer-based risk assessment systems

There are numerous examples of computer-based risk assessment systems. The important points to be considered when selecting such an option, are:

- Will it fulfil the organisation's needs?
- Is it flexible enough for us to be able to use it to carry out our risk assessment programme without having to utilise other more traditional methods as well?
- How difficult is it to operate, bearing in mind that we wish to involve those close to the action?
- How long will it take to train them in its use?

Risk rating

A factor common to all systems is the need for some means of rating the risks assessed so as to allocate priorities for action (and available budget). A number of these feature the simple concept of applying **low, medium** or **high** to the assessed risk and thus treating the 'highs' first and so on. This will be perfectly adequate for most organisations which in general are fairly low risk environments.

Due to the nature of their processes some organisations have a number of inherent risks of varying severity which need to be classified and managed accordingly. Also many managers are more comfortable with **numerical rating systems**. These are many and varied but have a common theme of:

- applying numbers to gradations of the severity of hazard potential, and numbers to the gradations of the severity and likelihood of realisation of risk;
- rating these numerical factors in a given circumstance;
- multiplying these factors together to give a rating.

Points to bear in mind when designing or choosing such a system are not to have too large a scale of gradation for hazard and risk. This will only confuse those attempting to use the system and lead to

TEAM-BASED RISK ASSESSMENT FORM

Carried out by....................................... **Date........................**

Description of activity/situation/process

KEY STAGES	HAZARDS PRESENT	RISKS	L	M	H	CONTROLLING ACTION

ACTION REQUIRED	
DATE REQUIRED	**DATE MONITORED**
COST - BENEFIT ESTIMATES	**MONITORED BY**

Figure 6.2 *Team-based risk assessment form*

inconsistent results. Some people have an aversion to numbers and this could get in the way of successful risk assessment. Simple systems work.

Risk assessment method, rating severity and likelihood

Many people who have carried out risk assessments have experienced some difficulty with rating risks. This difficulty centres on the assessors focusing on the potential severity of harm to be suffered from a hazard and not realistically assessing the likelihood of the risk being realised and marking everything as high risk.

What needs to be done is to make separate judgements of the level of severity of harm (injury or illness) and the likelihood of the risk being realised. The method shown in the form of Figure 6.3 overcomes these rating difficulties.

Scoring system

The rating system from the form shown in Figure 6.3 is as follows:

Severity (Sev)		1–5 Severity
Likelihood (Lik)		1–5 Likelihood
Severity × Likelihood	=	Safety factor

Assessments

15–25	High (H)
7–14	Medium (M)
1–6	Low (L)

Severity (Sev)	×	Likelihood (Lik)
1. No injury		1 Rare
2. Minor injury (No time lost)		2 Unlikely
3. Time lost up to 3 days		3 Probable
4. Time lost above 3 days		4 Very likely
5. Severe injury/death		5 Certainly

The form prompts the risk assessor to consider the hazards, check whether existing controls are adequate or should more be done. The residual risk is then assessed for severity and likelihood, scores (ratings) are awarded and safety factor produced. Using the resultant numerical rating, the risk can be rated as low, medium or high.

Risk assessment-based health and safety management process

Taking into account the definitions and requirements of the various regulations and looking at current best practice, we have designed a

SPECIFIC LOCATION:		DATE ASSESSED:	
ASSESSOR:		REVIEW DATE:	
TIME OF DAY:			
COMPILED BY:		COPIES SENT TO:	

SCORING SYSTEM
Severity (Sev) 1-5 Severity
Likelihood (Lik) 1-5 Likelihood

Severity x Likelihood = Safety Factor

Assessments

15-25	High (H)
7-14	Medium (M)
1-6	Low (L)

Severity (Sev)	x	Likelihood (Lik)
1. No Injury		Rare
2. Minor Injury (No time Lost)		Unlikely
3. Time Lost up to 3 days		Probable
4. Time Lost above 3 days		Very Likely
5. Severe Injury/Death		Certainly

HAZARD	EXISTING CONTROLS	RISK	PERSONNEL INVOLVED			RISK FACTOR			ADDITIONAL RECOMMENDED ACTION	ACTION TIME	BY WHOM	ACTION TAKEN
				Sev	Lik	L	M	H				

COMMENTS:	Do staff know who their Fire Marshalls/First Aiders are? Are staff aware of The Organisation's Health & Safety Policies & Procedures?

Figure 6.3 *Risk assessment*

risk assessment-based health and safety management process which can be used as a good set of general principles in carrying out the risk assessments. This should be suitable for most organisations and enable legal compliance, but more importantly it is practical. It must be stressed however that there is no model that is suitable for all types of organisations. Whatever system is decided upon will need 'customising' to suit the needs of the organisation.

The process

1 Look at what is actually going on or what is actually present in the workplace
This means walking the job, observing, talking and listening to people. For instance, what is the normal work activity? Is it what is stated in the operating manual or has there been some 'drift'? What happens in pressure/abnormal situations?

2 Look for any hazards
Look for anything with the potential to cause harm to people. Get the people working in that environment to help with this. Those closest to the 'action' are in the best situation to know what really goes on. Rate the severity of the hazard. Record the findings.

3 Do these hazards represent any risk?
Are the hazards adequately controlled, or should more be done to prevent the 'potential to cause harm' being realised? What is the severity of the risk? How many people could be affected? Who are they? Do not forget risks to visitors, contractors, customers, etc. Again it is vital that those who work in the area or use the equipment/methods are fully involved.

Consider what might present a risk to any particularly vulnerable people, such as new or expectant mothers. Record the findings.

4 Design safe systems of work
Design protective and preventative measures to eliminate or adequately control any risks. Using the team approach to do this is again vital. People will support what they have had a hand in creating. People are ingenious. This is an excellent opportunity to tap the talent that undoubtedly exists. The result is often not only a safer method of working but also an improvement of service, efficiency and effectiveness.

5 Implement the safe system of work
This is a vital stage, which is often handled poorly. Implementation

will need education, communication, commitment and enthusiasm or it will not be effective. Avoid the 'fine words in filing cabinets' syndrome at all costs.

6 Monitoring
Is it happening? As in item one above, walk the job, talk and listen to people. Look for evidence that the safe systems are being used.

7 Evaluation
Is the safe system of work achieving the objective it was designed for? Is there any residual risk?

Take measurements of health and safety performance. Have there been changes? Are all the factors taken into account in the original risk assessment still present? If so then the risk assessment process above should be repeated.

How to start a risk assessment programme

Many people have had difficulty knowing how to begin a risk assessment programme. After talking to several different types of organisation, we have the following suggestions to make:

- A senior manager should be made responsible for the introduction of the risk assessment programme. It should be a personal target for that manager, whose performance should be measured in this area as it would for other business activities.
- A risk assessment policy should be discussed and agreed upon. It should involve every member of staff and should form part of the organisation's Health and Safety at Work policy. The methods to be used in the organisation should be defined, the paperwork system selected, etc. Everyone should be briefed as to what they have to do. This could well be an item for team briefing.
- It could be useful to adopt a 'model' system, suitably customised to suit the organisation, but be very wary of making what you do fit the model and not vice versa.
- Managers should receive appropriate training in health and safety responsibilities and risk assessment techniques.
- Managers should be measured on their health and safety performance.
- All those who are taking part in carrying out risk assessments should receive appropriate training.
- A programme for carrying out risk assessments in the organisation, with dates and targets and allocation of responsibilities, should be agreed and published.
- The progress of the risk assessment programme should be

monitored via the safety committee as well as the managerial monitoring system.

Rough risk assessment

The decisions on priorities for risk assessment may well come from using a process such as rough risk assessment. This process typically consists of:

1. Gathering the available evidence, surveying the work areas, from accident statistics, accident reports, near miss reports, talking to staff about what they regard as problem areas.
2. Compiling a 'what's happening list' for each department or section. Get a 'competent' person from each department to help.
3. Utilise some form of simple recording system. This process is about speed and simplicity, to gain a picture of what the health and safety issues are.

What to look at:

- people;
- equipment;
- workplace (environment);
- materials;
- procedures/operations.

What to record:

- the significant findings;
- the existing control measures;
- the population affected.

Having done this you can start the detailed risk assessment process by concentrating on those risks that are prominent in the organisation. The key to success in this early stage is actively to involve people at every opportunity, and by showing your commitment to the risk assessment process.

This will help to counter the negative effect of cynics who will, if given the chance, label this as yet another 'management flavour of the month'. Remember that once you feel that your risk assessment programme is complete, it is good practice to review your risk assessments on an on-going basis. This should certainly be done after any changes. It also advisable to review at least once in twelve months to ensure that the assessment is still valid.

The Industrial Society

The Industrial Society can help you to become more successful in health and safety management. We have a nationwide team of qualified health and safety specialists who also have an in-depth knowledge of managerial skills. Our approach is typically based on a four-stage process:

1. **Investigation**. We work with you to analyse accurately your needs, discuss possible answers to them and set objectives in the form of measurable outcomes.
2. **Design**. We draw together the components of a development package to meet your specific needs and address the objectives.
3. **Delivery**. We deliver the package, whether training or consultancy, using the most gifted and knowledgeable presenters.
4. **Evaluation/support**. We assess the effectiveness of the work that we have carried out against the predetermined objectives and provide ongoing support to help the organisation to develop its own answers.

References

HSE, *A guide to risk assessment requirements*, free leaflet IND(G)218L.

HSE, *The costs of accidents at work*, HSE HS(G)96 (ISBN 0 11 886374 6).

HSE: *Display screen equipment work: Guidance on Regulations L26* (ISBN 0 11 886331 2).

HSE, *Management of health and safety at work: Approved code of practice* (ISBN 0 7176 0412 8).

HSE, *Manual handling: Guidance on Regulations L23* (ISBN 0 11 886335 5).

HSE, *New and expectant mothers at work: A guide for employers*, HS(G) 122 (ISBN 0 7176 0826 3).

HSE, *Personal protective equipment at work: Guidance on the Regulations L25* (ISBN 0 11 886334 7).

HSE, *Successful health & safety management*, HSE HS(G) 65 (ISBN 0 11 885988 9).

HSE, Work equipment: Guidance on Regulations L22 (ISBN 0 11 886332 0).

HSE, *Workplace health, safety and welfare: Approved code of practice and Guidance L24* (ISBN 0 11 886333 9).

McGuinness, P (1996) *Risk assessment. A practical guide.* The Industrial Society, Birmingham (ISBN 1 85835 164 2).

7

Needs Assessment for Occupational Health

Kit Artus
Artus Associates

Introduction

Successful businesses give a high priority to occupational health and safety as an integrated function which is seen as being as important as quality, client satisfaction and loss control. Senior managers should demonstrate commitment to eliminating hazards and to controlling risks to ensure that employees are protected from occupationally induced disease or health risks.

Measuring performance

In both proactive and reactive monitoring the objectives are not only to determine the immediate causes of occupationally induced disease or underperformance but to identify the underlying causes and the implications for the design and operation of the health and safety management system.

Proactive measurement

The proactive approach to occupational health is to plan to eliminate health risks by the careful selection and design of facilities, equipment and processes or to minimise risks by the use of physical control measures. Where this is not possible safe systems of work and personal protective equipment may be required to control risks.

Occupational health risks should, where possible, be measured against predetermined standards. This reveals when and where action is needed to improve performance. The success of action taken to control occupational risks can be assessed through active monitoring and health surveillance programmes. This includes an evaluation of possible health risks that may be encountered in the premises, from plant and substances used or developed, and from the way work is completed.

Commitment to continuous improvement involves the constant revision of occupational policies, approaches to implementation and techniques of risk control. Organisations which achieve high standards of occupational health assess their performance by internal reference to key performance indicators and by external comparison with the performance of business competitors – benchmarking.

Reactive measurement

The common response to occupational health disease or a claim is to assess performance through investigation of the claim. This is the assessment of failure. The cost-effective approach is to identify hazards and risks and plan to eliminate or control – planning to prevent.

Auditing and reviewing

The important aims of effective occupational health management are to learn from all relevant experience and to apply those lessons. This needs to be done systematically through regular reviews. Reviews of performance may be based on data from occupational hygiene monitoring, absence analysis, health surveillance programmes activities and from independent audits of the occupational health service and its systems. This is the basis of self-regulation and for compliance with Sections 2 to 6 of the Health and Safety at Work etc. Act 1974.

The inclusion of occupational health in other business areas

The recognition of occupational health in the following business areas are key steps to developing an occupational health culture:

- corporate strategy and social responsibility;
- finance;
- human resources;
- marketing, product design and product liability;
- manufacturing, distribution and operating policy;
- information management and systems.

Corporate strategy and social responsibility

Including occupational health in the business mission, philosophy and codes of ethics can be a means of developing the caring company image within the community. We have entered the era where it is recognised that the occupationally induced diseases have overtaken safety issues in terms of cost to employers, employees and society.

Occupational health needs the application of managerial professionalism as any other management issue. The inclusion of progress to the improvement of health at work in annual reports can further demonstrate that people are a valued resource to the organisation.

Finance

Occupational disease costs both employers and employees. The development of systems of loss control and cost reduction strategies for health at work is a move toward non-speculative risk management, for example, considered along with product liability, security, property damage, consequential financial losses and legal liabilities. A prudent employer takes the decision to consider occupational health strategies in terms of risk management. Attention should be focused on risk reduction by reducing the risks as far as reasonably practicable, which lowers the level of risk retention. Risk transfer is another option, for example, to transfer the risk to another company or to accept risk and the resulting insurance premiums.

Occupational health risk should be a consideration when investment, business acquisitions and new premises, plant and processes are planned. Some businesses have found it is an expensive mistake to add health concerns after acquisitions, e.g. asbestos.

It is often stated that occupational health and safety is expensive. If it is included in general financial planning and budgetary control the direction is a planned and not a reactive response. There should be an occupational health and safety budget. If a piece of plant were to cost an organisation £600.00 per day to remain idle, it is safe to assume there would be planned maintenance and an attempt to ensure that the plant remains functional. How much does it cost an employer to have a skilled person off sick due to an avoidable illness? Take salary, Statutory Sick Pay, management time to find and train a temporary, additional supervision for the replacement; consider the efficiency of the temporary staff member, perhaps 60 per cent of a skilled and experienced person's output.

Human resources

The recruitment, selection, placement, transfer, training, development and learning for a competent workforce is an integral part of human resources. The inclusion of health screening and health surveillance programmes and training in health risks is an effective approach to risk reduction and control.

Like any other management challenge structuring the managerial responsibilities and organisation to promote a positive occupational health culture is essential. This requires consideration of work and job structuring to achieve participation and involvement.

Health promotion activities have received a great deal of publicity since the Health of the Nation initiatives. However, occupational health issues were not addressed. These can be and need to be covered by the employer if there is to be an informed workforce capable of co-operating through understanding the risks to their health.

If an organisation is serious about risk management there must be adequate involvement and status for occupational health services. The main objective is to establish an occupational health service which is integrated into other complementary functions within the organisation.

Marketing, product design and product liability

To be proactive the specification of products, plant, equipment and services should be decided following consideration of occupational health needs. There is a great deal of published information and support available, for example, national legal requirements, international requirements such as EC directives, and national and international consensus standards such as British Standards, American National Standards Institute (ANSI) and International Standards Organisation (ISO).

Manufacturing, distribution and operating policy

The design, selection, construction and maintenance of premises, plant, equipment and substances should incorporate the needs of health protection. The Health and Safety at Work Act 1974 is of assistance as it specifies the responsibilities of manufacturers and suppliers.

The design of jobs should include the application of ergonomic principles and appropriate strategies for risk elimination, reduction and control – in essence developing quality management for occupational health.

Information management and systems

If an organisation is to give occupational health a higher profile and maximise the benefits of a healthy workforce it is essential to identify data critical to the management of occupational health risk. This may mean the selection of appropriate performance indicators and the use of information technology in the collection and analysis of essential data. The inhouse data can then be compared with the Health and Safety Commission annual reports, published statistics and the results of benchmarking.

To keep managers and staff informed the publication of collated data directed to improving performance and risk reduction is of interest, not only stating what went wrong but also what went right. It is a requirement to communicate the results of occupational hygiene and health monitoring under the Control of Substances Hazardous to Health Regulations 1994.

Occupational health and legislation

Health and safety law is intended to be partly preventative, partly punitive and partly compensatory. The rules are an amalgam of contract, tort and criminal law. Statutory provisions are interwoven with judicial decisions, and, in recent years, Approved Codes of Practice (ACOP).

For employers who are preparing or revising their occupational health services a dip into health and safety legislation is a starting-point to establish needs. Each firm and organisation has its own unique problems and may be subject to specific enforceable standards and regulations. These variations make the task of preventing occupational induced injury and loss difficult and challenging for the employer.

The law is an ubiquitous subject and is not easy for an employer or employee to draw boundaries or keep abreast of changes. There is no obvious boundary between occupational health and health and safety or indeed non-work related health and safety generally. Road traffic, environmental issues and consumer protection all overlap with health and safety at work.

The ultimate objective of occupational health is to reduce occupational damage and losses to the employer, employee and the community by working within the health and safety legal frameworks.

Health and Safety at Work Act 1974

The Health and Safety at Work Act 1974 was designed to increase the awareness of occupational health and safety at work. The Act applies to people and not to premises.

The Control of Substances Hazardous to Health Regulations 1994 and the Approved Codes of Practice

Regulation 11 - Health Surveillance

Health surveillance shall be appropriate where employees are exposed to one or more specified substances and are engaged in specified processes. Health surveillance is also relevant if the exposure of employees to a substance hazardous to health is such that an identifiable disease or adverse health effect may be related to the exposure. Plus there is a reasonable likelihood that the disease or effect may occur under the work conditions.

Management of Health and Safety at Work Regulations 1992

Regulation 5 - Health Surveillance

A risk assessment may identify circumstances where health surveillance is appropriate. Health surveillance is intended to detect adverse health conditions as early as possible, to prevent further harm. Results can be used to assist in checking the effectiveness of the risk assessment and associated control measures. Individuals at increased risk, for example, with existing health problems or disabilities, may be identified, enabling their greater protection.

Health surveillance should be provided where the following criteria apply:

- an adverse health condition or disease is associated with the work;
- it is technically feasible to detect indications of the condition or disease;
- it is reasonably foreseeable that the conditions of work may give rise to the condition or disease;
- the results of surveillance are likely to assist in protecting the health of those exposed;
- individual health records should be kept; these can form part of an existing health or personnel record depending on the extent and the person completing the health surveillance.

Management of Health and Safety at Work (Amendment) Regulations 1994 (S.I. No. 2865)

Employers are required to carry out a specific risk assessment where women of childbearing age or new or expectant mothers may be at risk from a work process, working condition or physical, chemical or biological agent.

Manual Handling Operations Regulations 1992

Guidance Note – Individual Capability – making an assessment – refers, among other things, to the need to consider individual variation of capability which will vary with age, strength, and pregnancy.

The final important section refers to the employer responsibility to assess the risk of injury as unacceptable if the manual handling operations cannot be performed by most reasonably fit and healthy employees.

Health and Safety (Display Screen Equipment) Regulations 1992

Regulation 5 - Eyes and Eyesight

Before employees become users of display screen equipment (DSE) they have a right to request an 'appropriate eye and eyesight test carried out by a competent person'. Further tests may be requested at regular intervals and when a user experiences visual difficulties.

The Disability Discrimination Act 1995

One challenge for the employer is to focus on the capability of the applicant or employee to perform the available task/s or job/s within the working environment. In evaluating capability the employer will need to consider reasonable adjustment to the job and/or working environment, in essence identifying what the employee or applicant can do and what the employer can be reasonably expected to do to reduce the impediments to gainful employment.

Occupational health policies

The aims for occupational health policies are to assist the employer to minimise the risks to health which may be caused by work activities, environmental exposure and/or stress encountered within the workplace – risk control. The use of the risk assessment process can be key to setting priorities and objectives for hazard elimination or risk reduction.

Once the risks have been identified there is merit in implementing appropriate health screening and health surveillance programmes. The main objective is to select people who are capable of performing the various tasks as an integral part of recruitment and planning for non-speculative loss risk management.

In order to support the employer in the key objectives of appointing capable staff and ensuring their health protection, the occupational health policies should include 'Capability Criteria' for at risk employees and tasks. 'Capability Criteria' are standards for health as required for a given job or group of jobs. Some of these criteria have been set, e.g. large goods vehicle (LGV) drivers. Some can be set by an employer following advice from an occupational health practitioner based on experience and/or HSE Guidance Notes, particularly the Medical Series. The adoption of such policies can then assist to identify specific management actions needed to support and promote a positive occupational health culture.

Needs assessment for occupational health risks

Occupational health can be defined as the speciality concerned with the inter-relationship between health and work, for example:

- work and health – an employee working in a noisy environment having to complete detailed tasks and take crucial decisions (physical);
- health and work – a fork truck driver with poorly controlled epilepsy (physical), a food handler with acute diarrhoea (biological);
- work and health – a painter exposed to respiratory sensitiser (chemical);
- work and health – a secretary continuously working at a keyboard without taking breaks to allow recovery from muscle fatigue (ergonomic);
- work and health – a sales representative working to tight schedules, paid on commission, working away from home and driving for long periods (psychological).

Occupational health is concerned with the identification, evaluation, measurement and control of adverse health risks. These risks can be classified as chemical, physical, biological, ergonomic and psychological. The issue for a needs assessment is to identify the work activities and exposures that may cause occupational injury, impaired health or discomfort to employees. Then the health and capabilities of employees in relation to those identified risks need to be evaluated. If there is a risk of occupationally induced disease then health screening and surveillance may be appropriate as part of the employer's control strategies and statutory duties.

Signs or symptoms of occupational disease or injury caused by health stressors can take up to 20 or 30 years from exposure to diagnosis. It is this latent period that some may mistakenly interpret as meaning 'We have no occupational disease or injury, ergo we have no significant risks'. Most occupational health injury is not the result of a sudden event, as with most accidental injury. The development can be slow and in some conditions insidious.

Needs assessment for health surveillance may involve more than one procedure. It may include the regular inspection of readily detectable conditions by a responsible person acting within the limits of their training and experience. This could be simply checking the hands of food handlers for cuts, infection or dermatitis. If a condition is identified then the employee can be referred for a more in-depth health examination or assessment.

A more detailed assessment may be performed by completing enquiries about symptoms, inspection and examination by a qualified person such as an occupational health nurse.

The requirement for a medical examination may be a statutory duty such as required by the Asbestos Regulations. This may include clinical examination and measurements of physiological or psychological effects by an appropriately qualified practitioner such as a physician with a qualification in occupational medicine.

In some instances it may be appropriate to complete biological monitoring, i.e. the measurement and assessment of early biological effects such as lung function. This may be needed if employees are exposed to a respiratory sensitiser. Biological monitoring also includes the measurement and assessment of workplace agents or their metabolites either in tissues, secreta, excreta, expired air or any combination of these agents.

Needs assessment system

To complete an occupational health needs assessment some or all of the following points may be considered.

1. Has the extent of the hazard or hazards been identified and where significant, assessed or measured?
2. Where significant risks have been identified have these been reduced to a reasonably practicable level?
3. Where there are remaining risks are these significant or can they be further reduced?
4. Is there an identifiable health risk?
5. Can the health effect be measured or identified by assessment of signs and symptoms?
6. Have appropriate health surveillance needs been identified?
7. Has health surveillance appropriate to the risks been implemented?
8. Is biological monitoring required and are the tests and laboratories available?
9. Have employees received adequate information, instruction and training to enable them to work safely and protect their health?

In essence there are three basic steps to a needs assessment.

1. What are the identified health risks?
2. What controls are in place?
3. What are the occupational health issues?

Table 7.1 *Employees hand spraying a suitably diluted phenol-based disinfectant*

Identified health risks	***Controls***	***Occupational health***
Phenol can be absorbed through the skin.	Disinfectant diluted before issued to staff.	Training of staff and supervisors in risks of inhalation and skin contact.
Inhalation of aerosol	Gloves recommended for use.	Skin inspections, glove selection and training in glove use and care.
	Risk assessments under Control of Substances Hazardous to Health Regs 1994.	Relevant occupational health history and routine health surveillance.
	Consideration of alternative disinfectant.	Data management and advice to staff and managers.

Table 7.2 *Employees working in an area of noise above 90dB(A)$L_{ED,d}$*

Identified health risks	***Controls***	***Occupational health***
Noise-induced hearing loss.	Appropriately selected hearing protection.	Audiometry for exposed staff.
Isolation and additional risk created by the hearing protectors.	Compliance with Noise at Work Regs 1989.	Evaluation and publication of results of audiometry.
Ear infections, dermatitis.	Can the noise be reduced at source?	Examination of the ears.
		Selection and fitting of required hearing protection. Training regarding cleaning and maintenance of hearing protection.
		Routine health surveillance for staff exposed to noise. Advice to staff and management.

Table 7.3 *Large goods vehicle driver with history of chest pain*

Identified health risks	***Controls***	***Occupational health***
Sudden collapse at the wheel.	Medical examination as required to hold LGV licence.	Routine monitoring of health. Health education regarding life style, diet, and exercise. Evaluation of medication in relation to driving and alertness.
Working long hours.	Management systems to check licence and driving standards.	Consultation with GP or consultant.
Stress.		Consideration of change of job, reduction of hours. Recommendation to driver to inform DVLA of significant condition. Counselling. Advice to management.

8

Disability, Rehabilitation and Employment

Dr Nerys Williams
Consultant Occupational Physician

There are over 6 million disabled people in the UK – around 14 per cent of the adult population; 2.5 million disabled people are of working age yet many face discrimination in gaining and retaining employment, sometimes because of inaccurate perceptions as to their capabilities. A study undertaken by the Spastics Society (now renamed Scope) and published in the occupational health press found that able-bodied candidates were 1.5 times more likely to receive a positive offer of an interview for a secretarial job than candidates who disclosed that they were registered disabled and had a history of cerebral palsy, all other details being similar.[1] Such discrimination is negative not only for the individual but also for the company as people with disabilities are often skilled and highly motivated.

A study undertaken by the Institute of Management Studies looked at employers' attitudes towards the employment of people with disabilities: 10 per cent of employers thought that disabled people had high sickness absence rates – a belief not substantiated by research; 7 per cent were worried about customer responses to a disabled employee[2] – but with an estimated one in six adults having a disability this is not likely to be a real problem. When the Devon Careers Service asked employers who had disabled employees about their experiences, 93 per cent said that disabled employees performed as well as or better than non-disabled employees; 8 per cent reported that disabled workers had better or equally good attitudes towards work; 96 per cent rated their attendance as good as or better than the able-bodied employees.[3]

With seven out of ten disabled people developing their disability while in work, employers need to be aware of disability at all stages of employment. Workers in the field have tried for a number of years to assist employers by developing guidance on non-discriminatory practice in recruitment[1] (see Box 8.1). But now there is an additional reason why employers should review their policies and attitudes towards people with disabilities – the Disability Discrimination Act 1995.

BOX 8.1
Non-discriminatory practice in recruitment (after Floyd)

Employers should ensure that:

- **all job application forms are accompanied by notes indicating health standards;**
- **no questions about disabilities are included on job application forms;**
- **job applicants complete a separate health declaration form which is reviewed only after candidates have been selected, subject to satisfactory health;**
- **health declaration forms are inspected only by occupational health physicians, or those delegated or qualified to do so;**
- **rejection on health grounds is only possible after a medical examination.[1]**

Disability Discrimination Act 1995

The Disability Discrimination Act 1995 (DDA) took effect on 2 December 1996. It replaces parts of existing legislation, notably the Disabled Persons (Employment) Acts of 1944 and 1958 that set the 3 per cent 'quota' of disabled employees which applied to employers with more than 20 employees and the Chronically Sick and Disabled Persons Act 1970 (CSDP) which required employers to provide parking, access and special sanitary facilities for disabled employees. With its associated regulations, the Disability Discrimination (Employment) Regulations 1996 and the Disability Discrimination (Meaning of Disability) Regulations 1996, the DDA introduces measures that aim to end discrimination against disabled people in the field of employment and access to services.

The DDA is implemented through the industrial tribunal system and applies to employers who have more than 20 employees. It provides for:

- the right of non-discrimination in respect of employment for disabled people;
- a duty on employers to make reasonable accommodation to working conditions or the physical features of the workplace;
- the disabled person's right of access to goods and services;
- the establishment of a National Disability Council to advise the government on disability issues.

Other areas covered by the Act include guidance for schools and colleges and on access and use of public transport.

If employers do not comply with the Act then employees (or prospective employees) have redress with procedures and time limits similar to those in race and sexual discrimination cases.

The definition of disability used in the Act is 'a physical or mental impairment which has a substantial and long-term effect on their ability to carry out normal day-to-day activities'. Impairment includes hearing and vision deficiencies and mental impairment includes learning difficulties and 'clinically well recognised mental illness'. Severe disfigurement is regarded as having a substantial adverse effect but tattoos or non-medical body piercing are not covered by the definition. Box 8.2. lists some 'normal day-to-day activities' included in the definition. A 'long-term adverse effect' is one which lasts for more than 12 months or is likely to last more than 12 months or for the rest of the affected person's life. The effects of medical treatment are disregarded when assessing the effects of impairment unless the treatment is likely to cure the condition.

Discrimination will occur if:

- the employer treats a disabled person less favourably, for a reason related to the person's disability, than the employer treats other people to whom the reason does not apply and the employer cannot show that such treatment is justified;
- an employer fails to comply with the duty of 'reasonable

BOX 8.2
Examples of some normal day-to-day activities included in the definition of disability

- **mobility**
- **dexterity**
- **physical co-ordination**
- **speech, hearing and eyesight**
- **ability to lift, move or carry everyday objects**

accommodation' (to the workplace or working arrangements of the disabled person) and cannot show this failure to be justified.

It is important for employers to realise that under section 59 of the Act they are not required to make any adjustment or do anything under the Act which would lead to a breach of other statutory obligations. This includes statutory obligations in respect of the health and safety of disabled people and other employees under existing health and safety legislation such as the Health and Safety at Work Act 1974 and the Management of Health and Safety Regulations 1992. The Department for Education and Employment (DFEE) has produced both a Code of Practice[4] and guidance on the definition of disability[5] to assist employers. An information line (tel: 0345 622 633, local rate, or text phone 0345 622 644) is also available whereby various leaflets on different aspects of the Act may be obtained.

In order to ensure compliance with the Act employers should review current practices and policies for recruitment and training and development including any existing fitness standards. There are relatively few legal standards of fitness which may preclude a person with a disability from a particular job but they do exist for seafarers,[6] pilots,[7] divers,[8] and large goods and passenger carrying vehicles, to name just a few examples. There are also industry guidelines such as those developed by the UK Offshore Oil Operators Association (UKOOA) for work offshore[9] but in the majority of cases no formal standards exist.

BOX 8.3
Light reading on the DDA

- **'Discrimination is bad news', *Occupational Health*, December 1995, 430–31.**
- **'Disability, discrimination and the law', *Occupational Health*, January 1996, 19–20.**

Assistance with adaptations and workplace modifications

Employers and disabled people may benefit from the Access to Work scheme – a government initiative which aims to provide practical help and advice. The scheme can pay for a range of services and equipment such as a communicator for people who have a hearing impairment, for adaptations to existing equipment or to a car and for alterations to premises or a working environment so that an employee with a disability can work there. Each applicant will be able to receive help to the value of £21,000 per person over five years, although if any adaptations or help bring more general benefits to the business then employers may be asked to contribute towards the costs. Further information and practical advice on the placement of people with disabilities can be obtained from Disability Employment Advisers (DEAs) who are based in local job centres and whose advice is free of charge for employers.[10]

Rehabilitation

Occupational rehabilitation may be necessary following prolonged sickness absence or after a relatively short absence for an occupationally acquired condition. Essentially the aim is to return the individual to their full capabilities and this can be achieved through grading their return, a technique known in the USA, as 'work hardening'. Rehabilitation should begin a long time before the individual actually returns to work. It is good practice for the employer, with the employee's permission, to establish contact with the GP at an early stage if absence is likely to be lengthy or if the return to work could potentially cause problems. An example might be in the case of repetitive strain injury (RSI) where the employer is unsure which activities the employee can do safely. Under these circumstances a return to modified duties or to reduced working hours initially may lead to the employee returning to work earlier than if they had to be fully fit. Employers are sometimes naturally concerned about how fit an employee is to do a specific job. In these circumstances it is beneficial for them to seek advice from a trained occupational physician. This is a doctor who has undergone training in all aspects of occupational health and is able to advise companies on fitness issues, legal requirements under health and safety law and occupationally acquired conditions and is able to develop rehabilitation protocols and monitor an individual's progress. Such doctors can be difficult to identify. See Box 8.4 for further details.

BOX 8.4
Occupational health advisors

For details of qualifications and contacts for occupational health advice, send an A5 SAE and two second-class stamps to:

'Occupational Physicians'
12 Brueton Avenue
Solihull
B91 3EN

Encouraging individuals to return to work mid-week rather than on a Monday may also facilitate successful rehabilitation as they have a natural break and rest after only one or two days instead of five. Descriptions to managers such as 'light duties' should be avoided as they do not make clear whether they mean 'no heavy lifting', 'no stress' or 'no physical exertion'. Instead managers need to know what an individual is capable of doing and what, if anything, they should avoid. This can be achieved by the company outlining the job and its requirements to the GP so that correct decisions can be made about rehabilitation and return to work.

This chapter is intended to give general information and is not a substitute for legal or medical advice which should be sought by companies and their personnel advisors.

References

1 Floyd, M (1995) 'Pre-employment screening and disabled people', *Occupational Health Review*: 32–6.

2 Institute of Management Studies (1993). Study by University of Sussex, reported in *Intacity Magazine* (1995).

3 Devon Careers Service (1990) *Employment Survey*, reported in *Intacity Magazine* (1995).

4 Department for Education and Employment (1996) *Code of Practice for the Elimination of Discrimination in the Field of Employment against Disabled Persons or Persons who have a Disability*, HMSO, London.

5 Department for Education and Employment (1996) *Guidance on Matters to be taken into Account in Determining Questions Relating to the Definition of Disability*, HMSO, London.

6 The Merchant Shipping (Medical Examination) Regulations 1983. SI 1983. No. 808.

7 Diving Operations at Work Regulations 1981. SI 1981. No. 399 (Regulation 7(1)c relates to the need for a certificate of medical fitness to dive).

8 International Civil Aviation Organisation (1985) *Manual of Civil Aviation Medicine*, 2nd edn, International Civil Aviation Organisation, Montreal.

9 Department for Employment (1994) *Access to Work*, PCL6, HMSO, London.

10 UK Off-shore Oil Operators Association (1992) *Medical Aspects of Fitness for Off-shore Work. A Guide for Examining Physicians*, UKOOA, London.

PART THREE

COMMON WORKPLACE CAUSES OF EMPLOYEE ILL HEALTH

9

The Scale of Work-related Ill Health

Trevor Benn
Health and Safety Executive

Introduction

There is no single source of statistics on the scale of work-related ill health. Part of the problem of quantification relates to difficulties in definition. Some diseases such as pneumoconiosis are clearly occupational since they do not in practice occur except when caused by workplace exposure. Others like back problems and chronic bronchitis can be caused by occupational or by non-occupational factors, or by a combination of the two. Cases whose causation is mixed are better termed work-related. There are a number of main sources of information, with different characteristics in terms of their completeness, coverage and reliability. Those that are cited here are described in more detail in Appendix I.

Population surveys

The broadest perspective of work-related ill health is obtained by asking samples of the population, workers and former workers, about conditions which they believe were caused or made worse by their work. The following national estimates were calculated from responses to a 'trailer' questionnaire which was attached to the 1990 Labour Force Survey (LFS).

- There was a total of 2.2 million cases of work-related illness in England and Wales in a 12-month period (nearly 6 per cent of the adult population). Of these cases 1.3 million were considered to be 'caused' by work. (Due to administrative reasons connected with the LFS it was not possible to ask Scottish residents about work-related illness at this time.)

- Not all of these cases were serious; in nearly half of the cases reported by people who had worked during the previous 12 months, they had taken no time off because of their illness.
- The 700,000 who had sick leave took an estimated total of 13 million days off work. An estimated 750,000 retired and unemployed people reported being affected by the longer term consequences of work-related illness.

A breakdown of the estimates according to type of illness, distinguishing those reported as 'caused' by work, is shown in Figure 9.1. Self-reported musculoskeletal conditions were by far the commonest disease category, with an estimated total of 593,000 cases 'caused' by work. Long-term consequences of trauma and poisoning, stress/depression, and deafness/other ear conditions each gave an estimated prevalence of just over 100,000 cases 'caused'. Other conditions commonly reported as caused by work were lower respiratory diseases (61,000) and skin diseases (54,000). The validity of self-reporting of work-related conditions was examined, as described in Appendix I.

Voluntary medical reporting and Industrial Injuries schemes

There are other sources of information in which doctors are involved in reporting or confirming cases of work-related illness. These consist of two voluntary reporting schemes called SWORD (for respiratory diseases) and EPI-DERM (for skin diseases) which are co-ordinated by academic medical units with HSE funding, and the DSS Industrial Injuries compensation scheme. Breakdowns of recent figures from SWORD and EPI-DERM are shown in Tables 9.1, 9.2 and 9.3 and figures from the Industrial Injuries scheme are shown in Table 9.4.

By the nature of these schemes, the cases reported under them will contain a higher proportion of the more serious cases than is found in the LFS self-reported cases. There are other reasons why these sources yield smaller numbers than the LFS. One is their more limited coverage; the DSS scheme deals only with specified well-defined occupational diseases ('prescribed diseases'), and reporting under the voluntary schemes depends on a case being seen by a participating doctor (see Appendix I). Another reason is that the figures are counts of incidence (i.e. new cases) rather than the prevalence estimates of the LFS.

Death certificates

Complete information of all fatalities caused by work-related health is not available. One approach is to look at mortality from specific

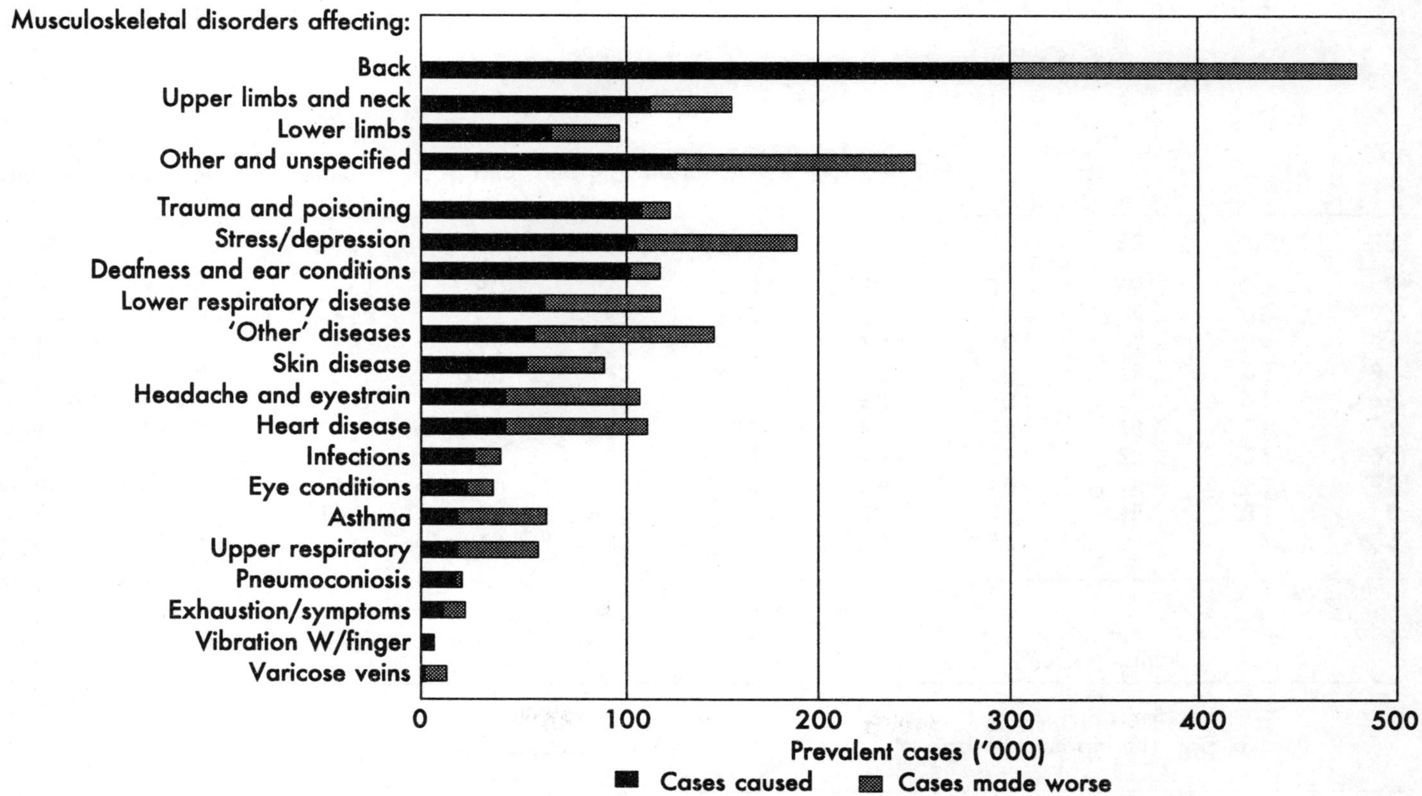

Figure 9.1 *Estimated 12-month prevalence of self-reported, work-related illness, by disease category, in England and Wales, spring 1990. Cases caused and cases made worse by work.*

Table 9.1 *Surveillance of work-related and occupational respiratory disease (SWORD), UK*

	Estimated new cases 1992–5				*Cases seen during 1995 by SWORD participants*				
						Age distribution %			
	1992	*1993*	*1994*	*1995*	*% male*	*16–29*	*30–44*	*45–59*	*60+*
Allergic alveolitis	97	115	48	20	78	22	34	22	22
Asthma	1047	912	968	851	65	21	38	33	8
Bronchitis/emphysema	133	60	38	50	96	0	15	23	62
Infectious diseases	53	51	59	31	63	13	29	29	29
Inhalation accidents	251	295	284	353	81	24	38	31	7
Lung cancer	146	63	70	62	97	0	0	21	79
Malignant mesothelioma	723	700	643	487	93	0	6	25	65
Benign pleural disease	681	766	735	590	96	0	3	36	61
Pneumoconiosis	418	385	342	172	94	1	4	28	67
Other	71	80	110	125	56	31	35	29	5
Total	3635	3456	3305	2741	80	13	22	32	33

Source: SWORD Scheme, National Heart and Lung Institute.

occupational diseases, though there are only a few of these that are life threatening and at all common (see Table 9.5). Another approach is to compare death rates for various diseases, both specific and common, in different occupations. This is exemplified in the analyses shown in the Registrar General's Decennial Supplement on Occupational Health.[1] The difficulty with this approach is that it is not easy to disentangle social and behavioural causes of variation from more specifically occupational ones.

Main occupational health hazards and disorders

The following descriptions do not attempt to provide a comprehensive review of all workplace hazards and occupational diseases, but give a very brief overview of some important hazards, especially those that can affect a wide range of occupations and industries, and where awareness may be inadequate in some areas. Fuller information is given in the annual publication *Health and Safety Statistics.*[2]

Diseases caused by hazardous substances

There is a legacy of disease from past exposure to substances (e.g. asbestos, coal dust and silica) which can cause long-term insidious harm, and where the interval between start of exposure and the diagnosis of disease is typically measured in decades. Thus, new cases of such diseases reflect the working conditions of the past. Occupational asthma and dermatitis are the main diseases that can arise from current exposures.

Occupational asthma

The LFS estimated that 20,000 people believed they had asthma caused by work, and a further 50,000 believed their asthma was made worse by work. Approximately 900 cases are reported annually to the SWORD scheme, and approximately 500 are assessed annually by the DSS, the lower number being probably due in part to a lower propensity to claim benefit among some groups of workers. Because the range of industries in which respiratory sensitisers are used is quite broad, and not all employees in those industries will necessarily be exposed, it is difficult to estimate with any confidence the total number of workers at risk. Among cases reported to SWORD in 1989–90 the occupations with highest incidence of asthma were spray painters, chemical processors, plastic workers, bakers, metal treaters, laboratory workers, and welders, solderers and electronic assemblers.[3] Figure 9.2 shows an analysis of the 1995 SWORD and Industrial Injuries cases by causative agent. Despite differences in coverage of

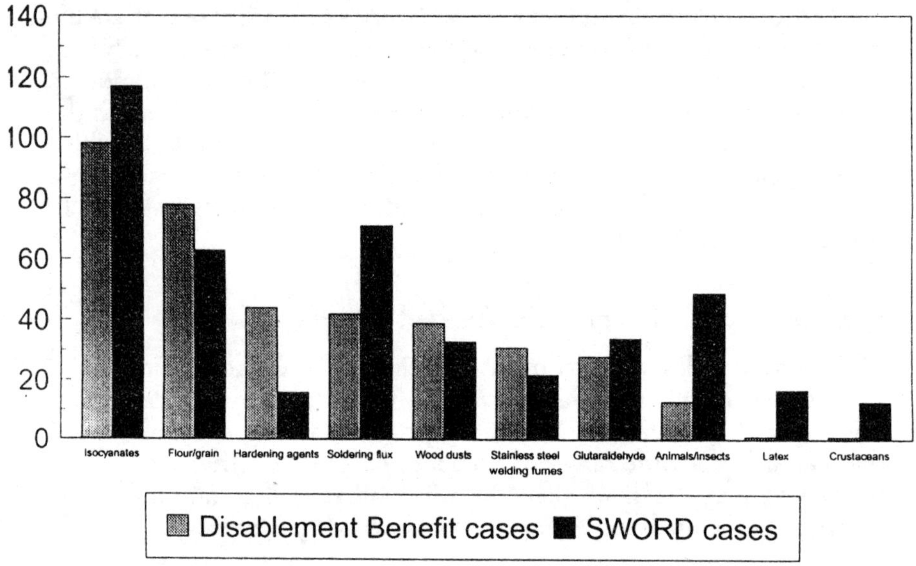

Figure 9.2 ***Occupational asthma, 1995. Disablement Benefit cases and SWORD cases by sensitising agent***

the two schemes, they present a similar picture of the most frequently implicated causes. Isocyanates, flour and grain, and soldering flux are among the leading causes in both.

Occupational dermatitis and other skin diseases

The risk of dermatitis caused by an allergic or irritant reaction to substances used or handled at work applies to a wide range of jobs. The LFS indicated a total of 54,000 cases of dermatitis or other skin disease believed to have been caused by work, and a further 30,000 made worse by work. Over 90 per cent of these cases arose as a result of a recent job (within the last three years) suggesting that occupational skin disease is not in general persistent. Among the recently employed three occupational groups had significantly above average self-reported skin disease rates, namely science and engineering, construction, and catering and hairdressing.

Among cases reported under the EPI-DERM scheme contact dermatitis is by far the commonest type of skin disease, making up approximately 80 per cent of reports both by dermatologists and by occupational physicians (Table 9.2). Skin infections are a relatively common diagnosis for occupational physicians, but are rarely reported by dermatologists. Skin neoplasia is almost always attributed to occupational sun exposure and is largely seen in retired men. Taking

Table 9.2 *Surveillance scheme for work-related skin disease (EPI-DERM). Reported new cases by type of disease, UK*

Disease group (c)	Dermatologists 1993 (a) %	1994 (a) %	1995 (a) %	Total period %	Occupational physicians Total period (b) %
Contact dermatitis	79.0	79.3	81.5	79.8	76.7
Contact urticaria	2.5	3.2	3.7	3.0	3.7
Folliculitis/acne	0.5	0.3	0.5	0.4	1.2
Infective	2.0	1.5	1.2	1.6	8.4
Traumatic	1.9	1.9	1.0	1.7	3.0
Nail(d)	0.8	0.7	0.5	0.7	1.1
Neoplasia	12.9	14.3	12.5	13.2	0.4
Other	2.5	1.2	1.5	1.8	6.2
Total cases	2433	1541	1444	5418	3176

Notes:
(*a*) Years from 1 February to 31 January.
(*b*) Period covered May 1994–December 1995.
(*c*) A patient may have diseases in more than one group.
(*d*) Dystrophy and paronychia.
Source: EPI-DERM University of Manchester Centre for Occupational Health.

all kinds of occupational skin disease together, EPI-DERM yields a 'lower bound' estimate of about 1.4 cases per 10,000 persons per year, for cases seen by dermatologists or occupational physicians.

Table 9.3 shows occupations with rates of contact dermatitis or urticaria greater than 5 per 10,000 per year, based on EPI-DERM. The high rates in coal miners and chemical operatives are due partly to the high level of occupational health provision in those industries. Most of the cases in miners were in fact reported by one occupational physician in a single outbreak of disease. Printers, machine tool operatives, foundry labourers and electroplaters have relatively high rates both in reports by dermatologists and occupational physicians and may be regarded as occupations with a raised risk. Among women, hairdressers and beauticians stand out in reports by dermatologists, laboratory scientists in reports by occupational physicians. The most common suspected causative agents for male cases include petroleum oils, soap and cleaning materials, cutting oils and coolants, and rubber chemicals (usually rubber gloves). Among women, dermatologists are more likely to report nickel, hair chemicals and food, reflecting poor access to occupational health services by those employed (e.g. in hairdressing and catering) in small companies.

Table 9.3 ***Occupations with high rates in reports to EPI-DERM. Cases of contact dermatitis and urticaria by sex, UK***

	Dermatologists (a)		*Occupational physicians (a)*	
Occupation (SOC)	*Number*	*Rate (per 10,000)*	*Number*	*Rate (per 10,000)*
Males				
Coal miners (910)	4	1.08	77	37.27
Chemical operatives (820)	76	4.23	222	22.23
Laboratory testers (864)	7	1.77	18	8.19
Printers (561)	46	7.46	12	3.50
Machine tool operatives (840)	119	5.36	92	7.45
Labourers in foundries (911)	10	6.19	6	6.67
Electroplaters (834)	12	3.38	10	5.07
Females				
Biological chemists (201)	5	1.03	34	12.61
Hairdressers (660)	364	11.87	11	0.65
Other natural scientists (209)	5	2.70	12	11.66
Laboratory testers (864)	8	2.06	24	11.13
Chemical operatives (820)	7	2.26	19	11.04
Spinners (812)	10	6.36	-	-
Beauticians (661)	41	5.43	-	-

Notes:

(a) Period covered for dermatologists February 1993–January 1996. Occupational physicians May 1994–December 1995.

Inadequately described occupations and occupations with less than 10 cases from both groups of reporters have been excluded.

Code numbers shown after occupation titles are from the Standard Occupational Classification (SOC).

Effects of asbestos, mineral dusts, and carcinogens

As noted above, there is a legacy of harm from past exposures to these substances, which are currently subject to strict controls. (See Table 9.4.) Asbestos can cause two types of cancer, mesothelioma and lung cancer. Because of the especially long latent intervals (up to 60 years), male mesothelioma deaths have been projected to go on rising for between 15 and 25 years, reaching a peak of 1300 to 3300 deaths annually.[4] However, controls on asbestos, and the reduction in asbestos usage have had an effect on the levels of mesothelioma deaths, which reached their peak for the generation born in the 1940s. Allowing for age differences, mesothelioma rates for those born in the 1960s have fallen to half the peak level. However, it is still necessary that all workers who may be exposed to asbestos, especially those in construction and related trades, are aware of the hazard and take due precautions. Asbestos probably causes at least as many cases of lung cancer also, but we can only estimate these, as they are individually indistinguishable from the much larger number caused by smoking. Because of this uncertainty, SWORD and DSS figures underestimate the true number of occupational lung cancers.

Similar uncertainties affect the estimation of occupational cancers caused by agents other than asbestos. There is a relatively small number of known occupational carcinogens, which are subject to strict controls in the workplace, if their use is unavoidable. Asbestos is by far the most important known occupational carcinogen. The best currently available estimate is that 4 per cent of cancer deaths have occupational causes (including asbestos), with a range of acceptable

Table 9.4 *Deaths due to occupationally-related lung disease, Great Britain, 1991–4*

	1991	*1992*	*1993*	*1994*
Pneumoconiosis (other than asbestosis)	287	274	281	276
Byssinosis	16	21	11	7
Farmers' lung and other occupational allergic alveolitis	8	4	12	10
Mesothelioma	1011	1082	1139	1235
Asbestosis (excluding death certificates which mention mesothelioma)	163	150	172	174
Total	1485	1531	1615	1702

Source: ONS/GRO(S)

estimates from 2 to 8 per cent (based on a review of American data, which is broadly applicable to Britain).[5] This would imply between 3000 and 12,000 deaths in Britain today.

Since the hazards of coal dust and silica are largely confined to industries where the dangers are well known, they will not be discussed at length here. Cases of pneumoconiosis (other than asbestosis) assessed under the Industrial Injuries scheme since the mid-1980s have shown a slight tendency to increase (possibly because of the contraction of the coal industry and a higher propensity for redundant miners to claim), but deaths due to pneumoconiosis (other than asbestosis) declined over the same period.

Acute poisonings and injuries from chemicals

In the five-year period to March 1995, approximately 80 per cent of the 12,300 cases of chemical injury reported under RIDDOR were in males. Around three-quarters of reported injuries were ones that caused more than three days incapacity for work, a further 23 per cent had specified major injuries, while fatalities occurred in only 1 per cent of cases. Half of the injuries were reported as burns, 26 per cent as asphyxiation or poisoning, and just over 10 per cent as superficial injuries.

The majority of exposures were to liquids (40 per cent), followed by gases in 18 per cent of cases and approximately 6 per cent due to solids or dust. In just over a third of cases there was a more detailed chemical code, and of these, gases (including carbon monoxide) accounted for one-third, acids and caustic alkalis caused one-fifth, and petroleum products and solvents caused 10 per cent. Approximately a third of the cases were in manufacturing or production. Other occupations where injuries were relatively common include maintenance personnel, labourers and managerial/administration staff, each of which accounted for 6–8 per cent of cases.

Illnesses resulting from inhalation accidents are reported to the SWORD scheme by participating chest and occupational physicians (see Table 9.1). The number of sufferers of such accidents stood at 353 in 1995, higher than the 250 to 300 cases seen in earlier years of the scheme. A special analysis of SWORD cases reported between January 1990 and July 1993 found that:

- chemical processing and engineering/metalwork were the occupations with the highest inhalation accident rate;
- of the 140 different agents involved in the accidents, 45 per cent were gaseous, 24 per cent organic chemicals, 15 per cent inorganics (including acids) and 6 per cent metal fumes;
- the agents most frequently involved in the accidents were chlorine (12 per cent of cases) and oxides of nitrogen (9 per cent of cases);

- persistent symptoms (usually respiratory) were reported in a quarter of cases.

Disorders related to physical, ergonomic and psychosocial factors

Major areas under this heading include musculoskeletal disorders, disorders caused by noise and vibration, and stress-related disorders.

Musculoskeletal disorders

The 1990 LFS trailer results show that musculoskeletal disorders were the most commonly recorded self-reported, work-related illness.

- The estimated number of cases 'caused' by work was 593,000 of which half (299,000) were back disorders; 19 per cent (110,000) were upper limb disorders (neck, shoulder, arm, elbow, wrist and hand complaints); 10 per cent (58,000) were lower limb disorders (hip, thigh, leg, knee, ankle and foot complaints) and 21 per cent (126,000) were other or unspecified sites.
- The average rates for workers who have been inactive for more than three years are higher than among the currently working, implying a substantial number of persistent cases.
- Occupations with a significantly raised risk of back disorders in the LFS included coal mining, nursing, transport and materials moving, construction and processing (metal and electrical). Coal mining, transport and materials moving and farming, fishing and forestry have significantly raised risks of lower limb disorders. Construction (men only) and repetitive assembly and inspection have a high risk of upper limb disorders.

Only certain specific work-related musculoskeletal disorders are prescribed under the Industrial Injuries scheme; they are mainly upper limb disorders (see Table 9.5). There was a total of 1108 assessed cases of these disorders in 1994–5 (excluding carpal tunnel syndrome caused by vibration, which is discussed in the section below).

Disorders caused by noise and vibration

Prolonged exposure to high noise levels can cause noise-induced hearing loss and tinnitus. The 1990 LFS gave an estimate of 121,400 people reporting work-related deafness or other ear problems. Numbers of new cases assessed by the DSS have been falling for some years, partly as a result of decline in employment in heavy industries (Table 9.5). (The DSS figures are of people who have a hearing loss of 50 dB(A) or more, which is quite a marked impairment).

Prolonged exposure of the hand or arm to vibration (by using hand-held vibrating tools, or by work such as holding a work piece against a

Table 9.5 *Cases of occupational disease assessed for Disablement Benefit under the Industrial Injuries Scheme, Great Britain 1992–5*

	Annual incidence Industrial Injuries Scheme[1]			
	1992	*1993*	*1994*	*1995*
Prescribed lung diseases				
Asbestos-related lung disease				
Asbestosis	354	418	376	427
Mesthelioma	551	608	583	685
Lung cancer (asbestos)	54	72	77	55
Bilateral pleural thickening	160	172	196	188
Other lung disease				
Pneumoconiosis (ex. asbestosis)	411	435	630	433
Occupational asthma	553	510	506	514
Bronchitis[3]	-	1560	2594	268
Other	20	13	11	16
Occupational deafness	972	901	882	763
Total lung disease and deafness	3075	4689	5855	3349
	Industrial Injuries Scheme[1,2]			
	1991–2	*1992–3*	*1993–4*	*1994–5*
Other prescribed diseases				
Vibration white finger	2369	1447	1425	1747
Musculoskeletal				
Tenosynovitis	649	911	800	787
Cramp of hand or forearm	52	116	135	116
Beat conditions	317	256	257	205
Carpal tunnel syndrome[4]	-	20	267	277
Dermatitis	411	419	392	368
Occupational cancers	23	30	44	26
Inflammation/ulceration of mouth[5]	75	494	528	589
Other prescribed conditions	36	36	40	43
Total other diseases	3932	3729	3888	4158

Notes:

1 Figures are of new cases of disease assessed at 1 per cent or more disability, except for occupational deafness, where they are cases assessed at 20 per cent or more disability.

2 Years from 1 October to 30 September.

3 Prescribed from 13 September 1993, for coal miners. The large numbers in 1993 and 1994 represent a backlog of existing cases.

4 Prescribed from 19 April 1993.

5 Inflammation/ulceration of upper respiratory tract or mouth. The increases from 1992–3 were connected with a take-up campaign by trade unions.

Source: DSS

grinding wheel) can cause hand-arm vibration syndrome. Vibration white finger, the vascular component of this syndrome, is a prescribed disease in specified occupations. Annual numbers of cases assessed by DSS have tended to fluctuate, probably as a result of factors which influence sufferers' propensity to claim benefit. Carpal tunnel syndrome caused by hand-held tools has been more recently added to the list of prescribed diseases.

Stress-related and psychological disorders

These disorders are undoubtedly a sizeable component of work-related morbidity, though in the absence of any DSS prescription or coverage by a medical reporting scheme it is difficult to quantify them except in terms of self-reported cases. The 1990 LFS estimated that 183,000 people in England and Wales believed that they had work-related stress, depression or anxiety, and that 105,000 of these believed the condition caused by, rather than made worse by work. This group of conditions represented the second most frequently reported after musculoskeletal problems within this survey. Groups with rates significantly above average included teachers, professionals, and other education and welfare workers. The difficulty with self-reporting of work-related psychological disorders lies in interpreting precisely what is being reported. Subjects' understanding of stress, such as perceived stigma or lack of recognition, may influence reporting of this condition and such factors could be related to occupational group or social class. Furthermore, the perception of suffering occupational stress may underlie the reporting of some other conditions as work-related, such as heart disease. However, if broadly defined as some form of psychological morbidity related to work, which could perhaps be characterised as moderate to serious job dissatisfaction, then most reported cases are probably genuine.

Notes and references

1 Office of Population Censuses and Surveys, Health and Safety Executive (ed F Drever) (1993) *Occupational Health: the Registrar General's Decennial Supplement* (Series DS no. 10). HMSO, London.
2 Health and Safety Commission (1996) *Health and Safety Statistics 1995/96*. HSE Books, Sudbury.
3 Meredith, S K and McDonald, J C (1993) 'Reported incidence of occupational asthma in the UK 1989–90', *Journal of Epidemiology and Community Health*, **47**: 459–63.
4 Peto, J, Hodgson, J T, Matthews, F E and Jones J R (1995) 'Continuing increase in mesothelioma mortality in Great Britain', *The Lancet*, **345**: 535–40.
5 Doll, R and Peto, R (1981) *The Causes of Cancer*, Oxford University Press, Oxford.
6 Ross, D J, Sallie, B A and McDonald, J C (1995) 'SWORD '94: Surveillance of work-related and occupational respiratory disease in the UK', *Occupational Medicine*, **45**: 175–8.

10

Occupational Asthma

Professor Anthony J Newman Taylor
Royal Brompton Hospital

Nature of occupational asthma

Occupational asthma is asthma induced by an agent inhaled at work. The defining clinical characteristics of asthma – variable narrowing of the bronchial airways – which distinguish it from other less reversible causes of airway narrowing – are manifestations of a characteristic (eosinophilic) airway inflammation. Agents inhaled at work can induce airway inflammation and initiate asthma by causing toxic damage to the airway epithelium (toxic inducers) or as the outcome of a specific hypersensitivity (or allergic) response (hypersensitivity inducers).

Toxic inducers

Toxic inducers are respiratory irritants such as chlorine, sulphur dioxide and ammonia which, when inhaled in sufficient concentration, cause airway injury and inflammation by a direct toxic action.

Hypersensitivity inducers

Hypersensitivity inducers include inhaled proteins (such as animal excreta, flour and enzymes), other complex biological molecules (such as wood resin acids and microbe derived antibiotics) and low molecular weight chemicals (such as isocyanates and acid anhydrides) which bind covalently to proteins to form hapten-protein conjugates. Airway inflammation occurs as the outcome of a specific hypersensitivity (probably allergic) response. Irritant induced asthma has no latent interval between irritant inhalation and the development of asthma, which occurs within hours of exposure; a latent interval of months or years is characteristic of hypersensitivity induced asthma.

Although the subject of increasing interest, irritant induced asthma is a considerably less reported cause of occupational asthma and to date the subject of less investigative interest. This chapter will focus on hypersensitivity induced occupational asthma which is the cause of the great majority of reported cases and has been the subject of considerable research interest. Indeed the term occupational asthma has been defined in UK for the purposes of statutory compensation as 'asthma induced by sensitisation to an agent inhaled at work'.

Causes of hypersensitivity induced occupational asthma

Some of the more important causes of occupational asthma are shown in Table 10.1. The proteins and complex biological molecules may be encountered in a wide variety of circumstances which include: agriculture; storage and transport of vegetable crops; food production; forestry; carpentry; use of laboratory animals; and the commercial exploitation of microbes as sources of food, antibiotics and enzymes.

Isocyanates are used in the manufacture of rigid and flexible foams, inks, adhesives, varnishes and paints. Acid anhydrides are used as curing agents for epoxy and alkyd resins. Complex platinum salts are essential intermediates in platinum refining and reactive dyes are used to bind a colour (chromophore) covalently to textiles.

Table 10.1 *Some agents responsible for 'hypersensitivity induced' occupational asthma*

	Proteins	*Low molecular weight chemicals*
Animal	Excreta of rats, mice, etc., locusts, grain mites	
Vegetable	Grain/flour, castor bean, green coffee bean, ispaghula, latex	Plicatic acid (Western Red Cedar), colophony (pinewood resin)
Microbial	Harvest moulds	Antibiotics, e.g. penicillins, cephalosporins
'Mineral'		Acid anhydrides, isocyanates, complex platinum salts, polyamines, reactive dyes

The SWORD (Surveillance of Work and Occupational Respiratory Diseases) scheme to which the great majority of respiratory and occupational physicians in the UK report new cases of occupational lung disease, has provided information about the relative importance of occupational asthma and its causes and has allowed estimation of the incidence of the disease in different occupational groups. The estimated incidence of new cases of occupational lung disease in 1992 was around 3500.[1] Asthma, which accounted for 28 per cent of cases, was the single most frequent diagnostic category.

Isocyanates have been consistently the most frequently reported agent, accounting for 22 per cent of cases; flour/grain dust, wood dust, solder flux and laboratory animals together accounted for a similar proportion (22 per cent). The overall annual incidence was $22/10^6$ working population. The occupational groups with the highest incidence were coach and other spray painters ($658/10^6$/yr), chemical processors ($364/10^6$/yr), plastic workers ($337/10^6$/yr) and bakers ($334/10^6$/yr).

Determinants of hypersensitivity induced occupational asthma

Three major factors have been identified as contributing to the development of occupational asthma in working populations exposed to its causes: exposure, atopy and tobacco smoking.

Exposure

Although the factor most directly amenable to control, exposure has to date received less attention than atopy and smoking as a determinant of occupational sensitisation and asthma. Nonetheless, several studies, both of incidence and prevalence of sensitisation and asthma (measured as work-related respiratory symptoms or measurable airway hyper-responsiveness or both) have found evidence for an exposure–response gradient. For example, the development of skin test reactions Alcalase, in enzyme detergent works to *B. subtilis* enzyme, primarily occurred during the first two years of exposure, with the highest incidence among those most heavily exposed.[2]

In a study of manufacturers of the pharmaceutical cimetidine Coutts *et al.* found the prevalence of work-related nasal and lower respiratory symptoms increased with increasing frequency of exposure to cimetidine at work.[3]

Atopy

Atopy, the tendency to produce specific IgE to common environmental allergens is usually defined in immunological terms as one or more skin test reactions to common inhalant allergens (which in the

UK would include grass pollen, *D. pteronyssinus* and cat fur). It is associated with an increased frequency of sensitisation and asthma caused by several agents, notably laboratory animals, enzymes and platinum salts. Several studies have found asthma to be some five times more common in atopic than non-atopic laboratory animal workers.[4,5] The incidence of skin test reactions was greater in atopic individuals to *Alcalase* in enzyme detergent workers in each category of exposure[2] and to the complex platinum salt ammonium hexachloroplatinate in platinum refinery workers.[6] On the other hand, for several of its causes, such as isocyanates, colophony and plicatic acid, occupational asthma occurs no more frequently among atopics than non-atopics.

Tobacco smoking

Tobacco smoking is associated with an increased risk of specific IgE and asthma in those exposed to several, but not all, of the causes of occupational asthma.

Specific IgE either measured in serum or inferred from an immediate skin test response has been found some four to five times more frequently in smokers than non-smokers exposed to TCPA,[7] green coffee bean and ispaghula,[8] and ammonium hexachloroplatinate.[9] The risk of developing asthma is also increased although less among smokers: all seven cases of asthma caused by TCPA in one factory outbreak were smokers[10] and the risk of asthma in a platinum refinery[11] was some twofold greater in smokers than non-smokers.

Diagnosis of occupational asthma

Accurate and early diagnosis of cases of occupational asthma is important. Remission of respiratory symptoms and restoration of normal lung function including non-specific airway responsiveness, can follow avoidance of exposure to the specific initiating cause. Furthermore, chronic asthma is more likely to develop in those who remain exposed to the initiating cause after the onset of symptoms.

The diagnosis of occupational hypersensitivity asthma is usually suggested by the history. It generally occurs in an individual exposed at work to an agent recognised to cause occupational asthma and only develops after an initial symptom-free period when the patient has been exposed without symptoms to the concentrations which now provoke his asthma.

Respiratory symptoms, particularly shortness of breath, wheezing, chest tightness and cough, occur during the working week, increase in severity as the week progresses, and improve during absences from work, sometimes at weekends and usually during holidays. The patient may also be aware of others who have developed similar respiratory symptoms at the place of work.

Outcome of occupational asthma

Asthma induced by an agent inhaled at work may become chronic, persisting for several years, if not indefinitely, despite avoidance of exposure to its initiating cause. This seems particularly, although not exclusively, to occur with asthma caused by low molecular weight chemicals. Asthma caused by agents such as isocyanates, acid anhydrides, and Western Red Cedar has been reported to persist for several years after avoidance of exposure in more than half of cases.

The important determinant of persistence of occupational asthma is duration of exposure to the initiating cause after the onset of respiratory symptoms. When examined, on average four years after avoidance of exposure, 60 per cent of 136 cases of asthma caused by Western Red Cedar (*Thuja plicata*) continued to have asthma. The interval from onset of symptoms to diagnosis was on average two and a half years longer than in those whose symptoms had resolved.[12]

Management of occupational asthma

Management advice for patients with occupational asthma has been greatly influenced by the results of studies of outcome of occupational asthma which have found evidence of relationship between the duration of symptomatic exposure and the risk of chronic asthma. The message from these studies has seemed to be clear:

- recognise occupational asthma as early as possible;
- identify its cause with reasonable certainty;
- avoid exposure as soon as possible.

The importance of accurate identification of the specific cause cannot be over-emphasised. Avoidance of exposure often involves relocation or loss of current employment. In the current economic situation, such a step without adequate reason could be the cause of considerable unnecessary hardship. Misdiagnosis of occupational asthma can be as hazardous for individual patients as missing the diagnosis.

Unfortunately, environmental changes, unless they involve substitution, are in general rarely able to reduce exposures sufficiently to prevent continuing airway responses in sensitised individuals.

Patients who develop occupational asthma when a specific cause is identified should be advised to avoid further exposure to the cause of their asthma. This seems particularly important where low molecular weight chemicals, such as isocyanates, plicatic acid or acid anhydrides, are the cause. These are particularly, although not exclusively, associated with the development of chronic asthma and airway hyper-responsiveness.

Avoidance of further exposure may require a change or loss of job, which for social or financial reasons, may not be possible. A change of occupation can be particularly difficult for highly trained individuals, such as experimental scientists whose livelihood depends on their knowledge and experience of working with laboratory animals. Such individuals and others sensitised to biological dusts who are unable, at least in the short term, to change their jobs, should be advised to minimise organic dust exposure, and to wear respiratory protection, most conveniently laminar flow equipment, when in contact with the organic dust. In addition, background prophylaxis such as sodium cromoglycate can reduce the risk of the provocation of asthma by indirect allergen contact, as from dust on colleagues' clothing. Nonetheless, it should be emphasised that such measures are temporary and, in the longer term, the means should be sought to avoid exposure to the cause of asthma.

When an individual does remain in employment exposed to the cause of his asthma, either directly or indirectly, the effectiveness of relocation or of respiratory protection needs to be monitored. This can be conveniently done by serial self-recordings of peak flow to determine whether or not asthma persists and if so if it is work related.

Prevention of occupational asthma

Reduction in the incidence of the disease will follow adequate control of exposure to its causes. Substitution of enzyme granules, of a size too large to be inhaled, for enzyme powder in the manufacture of enzyme detergents was followed by a marked decrease in the incidence of allergy and asthma to subtilisins;[2] substitution of a different paint for one containing TDI halted an epidemic of asthma in a steel coating plant.[13] Measures to secure control of exposure to the majority of causes of occupational asthma have, however, been impeded by lack of knowledge of the nature of exposure–response relationships for sensitising agents and inability to measure the concentration of airborne allergenic proteins.

Statutory compensation UK

Occupational asthma is a prescribed disease for 'employed earners'. The terms of prescription have recently been widened considerably. They now include asthma caused by exposure to 22 specified groups of agents as well as a 'w' category, which specifies 'any other sensitising agent inhaled at work'.

The current terms of prescription are shown in Table 10.2.

Table 10.2 *Current terms of prescription, asthma*

Disease	*Occupation*
Asthma	**Exposure to:** (a) isocyanates; (b) platinum salts; (c) acid anhydride and amine hardening agents; (d) fumes arising from the use of rosin as a soldering flux; (e) proteolytic enzymes; (f) animals including insects and other arthropods of their larval forms used for the purposes of research, education, in laboratories, pest control or fruit cultivation; (g) dusts arising from barley, oats, rye, wheat or maize, or meal or flour made from such grain; (h) antibiotics; (i) cimetidine; (j) wood dusts; (k) ispaghula; (l) castor bean dust; (m) ipecacuanha; (n) azodicarbonamide; (o) glutaraldehyde; (p) persulphate salts or henna arising from their use in the hairdressing trade; (q) crustaceans or fish or products arising from these in the food processing industry; (r) reactive dyes; (s) soya bean; (t) tea dust; (u) green coffee bean dust; (v) fumes from stainless steel welding; (w) any other sensitising agent inhaled at work.

References

1 Sallie, B A, Ross, D J, Meredith, S K, McDonald, J C (1994) 'SWORD '93. Surveillance of work-related and occupational respiratory disease in the UK', *Occup Med*, 44:177–82.

2 Juniper, C P, How, M J, Goodwin, B F J, Kinshott, A K (1977) 'Bacillus subtulis enzymes: a seven year clinical epidemiological and immunological study of an industrial allergen', *J Soc Occ Med*, 27:3–12.

3 Coutts, I I, Lozewicz, S, Dally M D, Newman Taylor, A J, Burge, P S, Flynd, A C, Rodgers, D J H (1984) 'Respiratory symptoms related to work in a factory manufacturing cimetidine tablets', *Br Med J*, 288:14–18.

4 Slovak, A J M, Hill, R N (1981) 'Laboratory animal allergy: A clinical survey of an exposed population', *Br J Ind Med*, 38:38–41.

5 Venables, K M, Tee, R D, Hawkins, E R, Gordon, D J, Wale, C J, Farrer, N M, Lam, T H, Baxter, P J, Newman Taylor, A J (1988) 'Laboratory animal allergy in a pharmaceutical company', *Br J Ind Med*, 455:660–66.

6 Dally M D, Hunter, J V, Hughes, E G, Stewart, M, Newman Taylor, A J (1980) 'Hypersensitivity to platinum salts: a population study', *Am Rev Respir Dis*, 121:230a.

7 Venables, K M, Topping, M D, Howe, W, Luczynska, C M, Hawkins, R, Newman Taylor, A J (1985) 'Interaction of smoking and atopy in producing specific IgE antibody against a hapten protein conjugate', *Br Med J*, 290:201–4.

8 Zetterstrom, O, Osterman, K, Machado, L, Johannson, S G O 'Another smoking hazard reused serum IgE concentrations and increased risk of occupational allergy', *Br Med J*, 283:1215–17.

9 Venables, K M, Dally, M B, Nunn, A J, Stevens, J F, Stephens, R, Farrer, N, Hunter, J V, Stewart, M, Hughes, E G, Newman Taylor, A J (1989) 'Smoking and occupational allergy in a platinum refinery', *Br Med J*, 299:939–42.

10 Howe, W, Venables, K M, Topping, M D, Dally, M D, Hawkins, E R, Law, S J, Newman Taylor, A J (1983) 'Tetrachlorophthallic anhydride asthma: evidence for specific IgE antibody', *J Allergy Clin Immunol*, 71:5–11.

11 Cartier, A, Malo, J L, Forrest, F *et al.* (1984) 'Occupational asthma in snow-crab processing workers', *J Allergy Clin Immunol*, 74:261–9.

12 Chan Yeung, M, MacLean, L, Paggiaro, P L (1987) 'Follow up study of 232 patients with occupational asthma caused by Western Red Cedar (*Thuja plicata*)', *J Allergy Clin Immunol*, 79:792–6.

13 Venables, K M, Dally, M B, Burge, P S, Pickering, C A C, Taylor, C F, Newman Taylor, A J (1985) 'Occupational asthma in a steel coating plant', *Br J Ind Med*, 42:517–24.

11

The Stress Factor

Caroline Toll
Human Resource Development

Introduction

It is becoming increasingly apparent that organisations, which means all levels of management, are expected to be responsible for the health and safety of their employees, both physically and now also psychologically. In some workplaces this is already part of the culture, but unfortunately it is not always the case. Where people are valued, given at least some control over part of their destiny and encouraged to fulfil their potential they are likely to be well-motivated, working well and feeling well in every way.

It is a sad fact that it has taken the threat of court action to motivate some organisations into taking the subject of stress seriously, instead of realising that looking after their greatest asset, people, makes good business sense. This is the result of the John Walker case where the social worker successfully sued his employers because, when he returned to work after a stress-related illness, they put him back in the same high pressure situation that had caused his absence in the first place. The high levels of absenteeism and illness due to stress reflect the sorts of pressures that people are being subjected to at the moment. Research in the Post Office[1] has shown that this could be reduced by two-thirds through the introduction of a stress counselling service, saving both financially and in human distress. This is not, however, the only remedy.

Definition

There are many meanings of the word stress and it is too often given a negative connotation.

STRESS
is a
RESPONSE
to the
PERCEIVED RELATIONSHIP
between the
DEMANDS ON US
and
OUR ABILITY TO COPE[2]

The mediating factor is the individual's perception. Demands or pressures, in themselves, are part of daily living. But it is the perception that varies: what is one person's welcome challenge may seem like the last straw to another individual. Healthy or unhealthy stress will result; which one will depend on the physical, mental and emotional state of the person at the time. What most people understand by 'stress' is either overstress or understress. The first means too many demands being made or pressure over a long period. The second means too little to do or not being stretched. This has implications for both individuals and managers. To understand more fully what is involved we need to look at the individual and then move on to the organisational aspects.

The employee

Physical reactions

Whether the demand is seen as welcome or unwelcome, there are certain hormonal reactions to the stimulus which are common. But the demand that is seen as a threat tends to invoke our primitive fight, flight or freeze response as the result of the release of adrenalin. This affects the parts of the body that help us to take action – heart, lungs, muscles, brain and liver. Other parts that would not be needed are deactivated – digestive system and sex organs, for example. These reactions at their best can save lives and, if well managed, can still result in healthy stress leading to high levels of motivation, achievement and satisfaction.

On the other hand, if the demands become too many and/or continue over a long period then the consequences can be serious. Our supply of energy is finite and can be exhausted with the result that our immune systems can become less effective. It is not difficult to understand why the stress-related illnesses follow logically on this process, related particularly to the parts of the body involved in the first place. It is important to recognise, however, that pressure may not be the cause of any of these disorders but it certainly has an exaggerating effect.

Other reactions

Much of the research has concentrated on the physical aspects of stress, but our thoughts, feelings and actions are also affected. In a sense the stress response is purely the result of our thoughts, both the initial recognition of the demand and how we interpret it. It will be most people's experience that we react in many different ways to demands made on us and the results.

Thoughts

When we are challenged in a constructive way and are willing and able to respond we think clearly and quickly, are creative and motivated to work to the best of our ability. This is healthy stress. On the other hand if it seems like a threat then we may not be able to think clearly, concentration will be poor and we can be confused. Obviously this is unhealthy both for the effectiveness of the individual and the organisation.

Feelings

When the demand is welcome then there is often a feeling of excitement and enjoyment in responding, particularly if we are achieving something and maybe stretching our potential. However, the unwelcome demand will leave us feeling down, possibly out of control and overwhelmed.

Actions

The state of our bodies interacts with thoughts and feelings and our behaviour is often the first sign of unhealthy stress. If the demands are appropriate to us as individuals and our ability to cope, then our work will be of a good standard and we will behave co-operatively. When the demands appear to be unreasonable we tend to find ways of avoiding or postponing the work. We are likely to be working below our capability as well as behaving with other people in an uncharacteristic way.

Signals

The first signs that someone is suffering from unhealthy stress will probably be things that makes you think 'I wonder why so-and-so seems different.' The person who is normally friendly and chatty sits staring at the computer. The person who keeps calm most of the time suddenly gets angry with people. The person whose work is usually accurate begins to make mistakes. Often we are aware in ourselves that all is not well but we think we are too busy to stop, work out what is causing our unease and then do something about it. In fact it is most likely that if we have let ourselves reach the unhealthy stress state then we have not much spare energy to take action that might improve things. A helpful manager or a friendly colleague may be able to help us to recognise when we need to do something about it. In Figure 11.1 the adaptation of the 'stress curve' helps to illustrate this.

At (1) we may be suffering from many of the signs of overstress because of frustration or depression. At (2) we are beginning to do our best work and are functioning effectively. At (3) we are beginning to show the signs of unhealthy stress. At (4) we are suffering from exhaustion and one or many of the stress-related disorders.

What you can do as an individual

As an individual there are many things that can be done to prevent becoming overstressed or to reduce stress levels that have become too high. These can help us to *train* to be stress fit and they offer us ways to deal with reactions in the body, thoughts, feelings and actions.

***T*alking** – helps us to sort out the issues and work out ways of dealing with them; also it offers an opportunity to express feelings and having them accepted by friends, colleagues, counsellors and/or acquaintances who can all be helpful.
***R*elaxing** – with short exercises for 'relaxation on the run' at odd times during the day; or alternatively outside work perhaps by reading quietly or joining a special stress management class. All can help to release tension and lower blood pressure, so we need to find one or more ways that work for us.
***A*ctivities** – help to keep us physically fit and release energy that has built up but not been used, perhaps by doing something active on our own or joining with others in a sport.
***I*nterests** – help to refocus the mind and give us a different perspective by concentrating on a hobby or course that interests us.
***N*ourishing** – helps to keep us physically fit. A balanced diet with plenty of fresh fruit and vegetables is best for most people, avoiding too much alcohol and caffeine. But there is an emotional type of nourishing that is equally important – try to build up the support of people who care about you and do something purely for your own pleasure at least once a day.

These are all areas that we need to consider if we are under a lot of pressure and they are all things that are within our control. It may be difficult to make the time but it is surely better to do something constructive rather than deal with the consequences of neglecting ourselves.

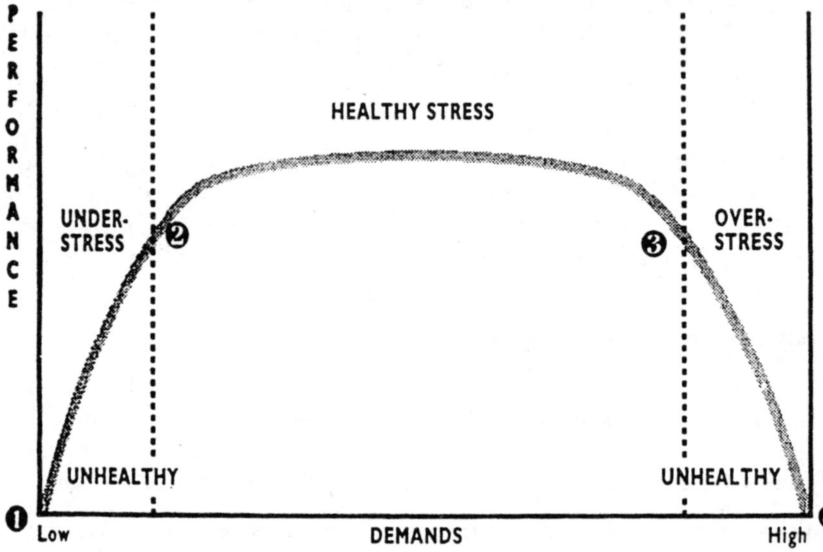

Figure 11.1 *The stress curve*

Organisational responsibility

Having looked at the individuals' responsibility towards themselves it is important to recognise that this may only be dealing with the symptoms and not addressing the causes of overstress or understress. The Health and Safety Executive's latest guidelines say 'stress should be treated like any other health hazard'.[3] It is not enough that short courses on stress management should be offered to employees, though these can be very valuable to individuals.

The subjects that appear most often on these kinds of courses as the sources of most overstress at work are constant change, lack of control, bad communication and overload. There is very often a combination of all four which can be devastating for the individuals as it produces fear, suspicion and rumour, as well as feelings of helplessness, disorientation and being undervalued. Consequently there will be loss of trust and motivation which will result in lowered morale and standards of work and an increase in absenteeism and stress-related illness. From a management and financial point of view this can be very damaging to any organisation.

The subjects we are considering here are all covered in best management practice and are directly relevant to the subject of stress.

Constant change

Constant change is a feature of modern life and it remains to be seen if the human being will be able to adapt healthily to it. Any change to the status quo can be seen as a threat to stability. For example, fear of redundancy and the feelings it provokes are not conducive to happy working relationships. This is where communication is so important because if people understand why a change is happening and on what criteria decisions are based they will be much more likely to be able to adapt co-operatively.

Lack of control

The feeling of being completely out of control of what is happening can be undermining to individual confidence and self-esteem. These are both personal attributes which are important for effective working. This is where there is a place for people to take charge of looking after themselves outside work, so that they can feel that they have some control over a part of their lives. However, this does not mean that management can abdicate responsibility for what is happening at work.

Bad communications

Bad communications can prevent people from understanding what decisions are being made and why. Increasingly organisations are also realising that they can benefit from hearing from people at all levels as to what their concerns and suggestions may be. This is part of good decision-making but it is necessary at the same time to communicate what is happening to people's ideas. If they can see that they are having some influence this will be a morale booster, but if the ideas cannot be used then people need to know why.

Overload

However, there comes a point when people are being asked to do too much for too long. There are endless examples of people suffering from overload, often being expected to do two jobs as a result of cuts. This cannot be sustained in the long run without damage to the person's well-being and/or to the standard of work.

Valuing people

Contrary to the perception of some, the reasons that people go to work are not only to earn money and it is not the only way in which they need to feel valued. A sense of achievement and companionship come high on the lists of many. Generally, it must be clear that encouragement, guidance and praise produce the best atmosphere in which people flourish and fulfil their potential. If this is not happening then the organisation will not be flourishing or fulfilling its potential either, particularly in the long term. It does not cost to recognise someone's special achievement or even to show that a piece of ordinary work has contributed to the success of the enterprise. Equally, it is important to support and encourage, with clear guidance, those who need to do better, rather than to lose their interest by putting them down or denying them the opportunity to improve.

Some people have troubles in their home lives which may be considered to be of no concern to the organisation. However, we cannot completely split ourselves into two and the influence on what is happening at work on home life, as well as the opposite, have a direct bearing on how healthily or unhealthily stressed a person is. Several demands on us may be manageable but if there are too many from different directions overstress is likely to result. Help and support in managing a situation such as this can come from a considerate manager and/or from support at home. They can both be crucial in helping someone to stay stress fit.

What you can do in management

- Develop a stress policy and make sure everyone knows about it.
- Make sure all managers are aware of the points discussed above and act on them.
- Where necessary offer training.
- Consider management practices in the areas where it may be possible to ease pressure points and make people feel valued – structure, management styles, communication, employment practice, job design, workplace environment, training, welfare services.
- Consider introducing a counselling service, either inhouse or external.

Conclusion

Stress and its implications are a huge subject and we have only been able to touch on the main aspects. Both management and individuals need to take overstress and understress seriously if we are to be fully effective as organisations, workers and people.

References

1 Cooper, C L, Sadri, G, Allison, T and Reynolds, P (1990) 'Stress counselling in the Post Office', *Counselling Psychology Quarterly*, Vol 3(1).

2 Warren, E and Toll, C (1993) *The stress work book: how individuals, teams and organisations can balance pressure and performance'*, Nicholas Brealey Publishing in association with The Industrial Society, London.

3 Health and Safety Executive (1995) *Stress at work: a guide for employers*', HMSO, London.

Can health be managed?

People are any organisation's primary asset. It follows, therefore, that employers should be interested in the health of their employees - be it because of an altruistic motivation of genuine concern for its personnel or a question of economics. The latest estimate is that occupational ill health and work related accidents cost Britain between £11 billion and £16 billion per annum as a result of lost production, damage to equipment, recruitment, retraining and compensation. At the company level these costs typically represent between 5% and 10% of annual profits.

With an average 3.5% of the workforce absent at any one time, the CBI estimates that the direct cost of sickness absence in 1995 cost British industry a further £10 billion, with the indirect costs of reduced competitiveness, reduced customer service and lowered employee morale an additional £6 billion. These figures provide a reasonable business case for further investment in the management of employee health, particularly when many of the factors driving this level of ill health are preventable, or at the very least modifiable.

There is a growing agreement, though, that the dividing line between absenteeism and physical sickness absence is not as clear cut as might have been previously thought, and that it is the management of employee health **and** well-being e.g. both physical and mental health, that can make the difference between high and lower levels of absence in general.

In a recent Institute of Management survey, 70% of employees reported that they believe their health to be adversely affected by job related anxiety. There is clearly an issue then about an organisation understanding the extent to which any or all of the factors that drive sickness absence and absenteeism are an issue for them, and having identified them as such, whether it is possible to do anything about it. BUPA believes that all of the health issues, and most of the less obviously physical or mental health related absences, can be influenced through the development of a formal strategy for health which increases focus on positive health management.

The BUPA Health Audit
Developed in consultation with a number of major organisations, the *BUPA Health Audit* consists of a number of diagnostic tools which enable the rapid quantification of the health status of both the employee and the workplace - what is the effect of health on work and the effect of work on health? The Physical health of the workforce is assessed using the well established technique of health risk appraisal through the completion of Health Profile Questionnaires, assessing each employees personal health risk from a combination of medical history and lifestyle factors. This can then be backed up with an analysis of company wide sickness absence data and a clinical audit of secondary care claims through the corporate medical insurance scheme. Mental health is assessed using a questionnaire based Stress audit, which seeks to identify, at both the individual and corporate level, the sources of pressure for employees and their individual coping strategies.

Over the past year BUPA has worked with a number of major organisations to help them better understand the payback from their current expenditure on health, and see where it may be possible to shift the emphasis into the areas of positive health management. Does it bring benefits? Those companies who have implemented all or some of the programme elements have reported that it does.

Good Health Means Good Business, and the financial rewards, as well as the human ones, are significant.

For further information about BUPA Health Audit and other BUPA Health Management initiatives, please contact Lesley Cooper on 0171 656 2238.

12

Musculoskeletal Problems in the Workplace

Geoffrey Laycock
The Otter Consultancy

Introduction

Musculoskeletal problems are not a new phenomenon. Gamekeeper's thumb, housemaid's knee and many others have probably been around for centuries. In the 1980s the term RSI, repetitive strain injury, came into common use, now usually replaced by WRULD or work-related upper limb disorder. Before showing two case studies with very different problems, let us not forget that it is not just upper limbs we are interested in. Back or spinal and lower limb problems must also be recognised and removed or controlled where they exist.

Legal duties on employers to take such action exist first in the Health and Safety at Work etc. Act 1974 and has been supplemented by more specific duties in later regulations. The Manual Handling Operations Regulations 1992 (L23) and the Health and Safety (Display Screen Equipment) Regulations 1992 (L26) are two examples.

While these conditions are not likely to be life threatening, they can represent considerable pain and disability for the person suffering from them. They will affect the ability of the employee to work at their best and hence everyone loses out. Development of a WRULD by an employee may result in time off work, reduced efficiency when at work, complete loss of a valued employee and possibly a legal case for compensation. According to the Labour Force Survey of 1993 there were 74,000 cases of RSI in England and Wales, 50,000 caused by work, 24,000 aggravated by work. In 1991 it was estimated that 2,300,000 days of certified incapacity were a result of RSI. Settlements have ranged from thousands of pounds to around £100,000. Despite all these good reasons for identifying and removing or reducing potential WRULD problems, often little is done.

There is an increasing amount of guidance available. In addition to the above two sets of regulations (with guidance) there is also: *A pain in your workplace* (HS(G)121); and *Work related upper limb disorders – a guide to their prevention* (HS(G)60). For work in the healthcare industry, *Guidance on manual handling of loads in the health services* provides a good starting-point.

The following case studies show some of the common problems with an office-based wordprocessor and the very extensive range of factors that may need to be looked at on a factory assembly task.

Wordprocessor workstation analysis

This example shows typical results from a display screen equipment workstation investigation where the user had been complaining of various aches and pains for up to four years. Full details of the results are not included, this being an illustration only of what can be found and what actions may be taken. The only way to make significant positive changes in this workstation was the replacement of the combined processor/keyboard/printer unit with a now more common PC or similar equipment.

A further significant finding during the investigation was the serious lack of safeguards on data. No back-up copies of documents or the numerous standard documents in use were kept and loss through any cause would have resulted in severe problems.

The analysis consisted of direct observation of the workstation equipment and location environment, use of a standard workstation evaluation questionnaire, a self-completion questionnaire for the user and by direct discussion with the user.

The basis of the analysis was the Health and Safety (Display Screen Equipment) Regulations 1992 and associated guidance, plus other guidance. The Regulations came into force 1 January 1993 with a time allowance for workstations in use before that date. For workstations in use prior to January 1993 (as this one was) the schedule to the Regulations did not have to be complied with until 31 December 1996. However, any risks to health or safety identified as a result of the analysis (required by regulation 2) must be reduced to the lowest level reasonably practicable without this time allowance.

Background information

One particular employee had worked in this location in the building for approximately four years. She was about 5′ 4″ in stature and ecto-mesomorphic. At about the time of the move to this work area she recalled mild aching to the back of the neck radiating up to the posterior aspect of the skull. After discussion with persons in the company the screen location was changed by removing the monitor from its native cantilever support. The monitor was relocated on a typical after-market cantilever support which allows a greater degree of movement and alternative location. At the same time a cantilever design of A4 document holder was provided.

Prior to the changes the screen was to the left of the Olivetti word-processor unit and documents being copied from were flat on the desk, again to the left of the wordprocessor. Such an arrangement is common and often can lead to pains in the neck or shoulders due to constant tension in the neck/upper back muscles. After the changes the monitor was located centrally behind the wordprocessor with the document holder to the left and slightly lower than the screen.

For the last couple of years there was some pain to the forearms and wrists. A height adjustable wrist rest had been in use for about one year.

Investigation

Two questionnaires based on the contents of the Schedule to the DSE Regulations were used. Such checklists are available from a number of sources and provide a structured approach to the investigation.

Overall, the workstation was typical office layout using a standard office desk. The Olivetti unit wordprocessor, obtained about 1991, was a combined processor and daisy wheel printer with fixed keyboard. This occupied considerable space on the desk and greatly reduced the possibilities for workstation adjustment.

The layout was reasonable given the above constraints and attempts had been made to provide equipment to reduce the problems. In addition a seat base wedge had been provided to improve posture but this should have been unnecessary as the seat base angle to the horizontal was adjustable. This was not known by the users.

Although environmental conditions were not ideal they were not considered to warrant any major changes.

Recommendations

1. The user of the workstation examined was given personal instruction in the correct method of adjustment, based on an introduction to the potential risks involved with not doing so. It was strongly recommended that similar information was given to the remaining users. A number of videos exist that satisfy much of the requirements.

Poor organisation of workspace and adjustment of chairs are common reasons for musculoskeletal problems developing.

2. A major problem was lack of space on the desk top. This restricted the amount of reorganisation possible. The ideal would be larger desks, at least 5ft by a depth of 4ft. Without incurring the expense of complete replacement, a single additional desk to allow additional space for both workstations in this location would have allowed much greater personal reorganisation. A side table of similar height to the desks would also have allowed considerable extra space and was a further option.
3. The further major problem was the design of the equipment, i.e. wordprocessor, in use. Where these combined units exist there is hardly ever the ability to adjust and organise to the best positions for each user. In the case of this workstation the available positions of keyboard, monitor and document holder were restricted.

   The best adjustments possible were made during the workstation analysis but the ideal solution would be replacement with either stand-alone PC-based systems or a networked server system with individual monitor/keyboard workstations. Either option would also allow the use of larger monitors with clearer displays.
4. The monitors in use did not allow adjustment of both contrast and brightness and would not comply with the requirements of the schedule at the end of 1996. While this was not considered to be a serious problem in the workstation examined, modern monitors have high definition displays, are very stable and the larger sizes allow much quicker working, especially when complex wordprocessing software is in use as would probably happen if the system was changed.

Domestic oven assembly

Background

This example shows the range of possible contributing factors to the problems that developed and extensive range of possible solutions.

Since the introduction of cooker assembly, a number of operatives had experienced and reported various musculoskeletal complaints. These included locations at neck/back/shoulders, arms, wrists or combinations.

During the previous year a number of changes had been made to the workstations, various component changes had been tried, different screw fasteners, screwdriver design, etc. It was in view of the improvements made but the musculoskeletal problems remaining that the investigation was called for.

Task description

Cooker oven assembly was carried out at six assembly stations supplied by conveyor feeders. The cooker internal structure was placed on a transit baseboard which was also fitted with a component box holding the remaining parts of the oven assembly.

At each station two operatives worked as a team. The most accomplished team was able to assemble about 50 units per shift while a new team still gaining experience was working at about 30–35 units. Extensive training of each team, of up to three months, was necessary to allow a flexible assembly line. They were able to assemble any model of oven required.

Although extensive training was carried out there were obvious differences in the final team organisation of assembly. Some teams had set tasks per person and did not vary from this regime, other teams would switch tasks. The most productive team had set tasks per person and worked in a highly co-ordinated way. This increased level of individual task practice would account in part for the higher efficiency, but would also tend to concentrate any potential problems from individual task elements.

Initial observations

From the observations of the assembly, and discussion prior to this, the following possible problem areas for investigation were identified:

- component design;
- component accuracy of fit;
- order of assembly;
- fastener design and ease of initial location then insertion, plus related component design;
- stability of oven assembly on transit board;
- height of assembly conveyor and assembly workstation;
- air-powered screwdriver design;
- individual adopted work posture;
- use of pinch grip for electrical connector insertion;
- team assembly organisation and task allocation;
- speed of assembly and rest breaks;
- type of gloves used;
- environmental conditions.

After direct observation of assembly a number of key issues were considered of primary importance, these were:

- the number and location of screw fasteners;
- the posture adopted for fastener insertion and its relationship to individual stature;

- screwdriver design relative to the location of the fastener, i.e. vertical or horizontal.

Actions

A three-stage action plan was proposed.

Stage One
This included:

1. Sorting out the problem of oven base panel distortion which made assembly difficult at times, resulting in excessive pressure being required to locate screw holes.
2. Revisit the screw fastener specification. Variation in screw thread root size has been identified as one problem with insertion.
3. Reduce the number of screw fasteners. This is subject to a BSI or BEAB approval for design change. If agreed the number of fasteners will reduce by 18, making a significant reduction to the problems created by location and insertion pressures.
4. Consideration of substitution of zero insertion force (ZIF) electrical connectors for some of those in use.
5. Reintroduce a pistol grip design driver for use with horizontal fasteners. This had been tried but using a modified, existing automatic straight driver. This was rejected because of operator dislike – probably due to weight and unwieldiness. A proper pistol design was needed.
6. Associated with the above, all operatives to be properly trained and instructed in which driver to use for individual fasteners, and the correct posture to adopt, i.e. hand orientation.
7. A check was to be made to see if the air hose to the drivers could be reduced in size to reduce the weight and resistance to movement.
8. The use of sliding rail or spring type hose supports to supplement the above was to be investigated.
9. BS5750 procedures had been written. Short additional instructions on assembly method, order and including items from above were needed.

Stage Two
A structured form of individual health monitoring was to be introduced. This would take the form of weekly or fortnightly questionnaires allowing pain/discomfort recording on body representative diagrams, and development of personal history.

Stage Three

Once health monitoring was in place, observation of individuals could occur. Individual problems could be considered in light of stature and build, work methods, team organisation and use of equipment. This stage would involve on-site direct observation, video recording of work activities, interviews with operatives, off-site video analysis and reporting.

13

Prevention of Occupational Contact Dermatitis

Dr Joanna M Wattie
Independent Consultant in Occupational Medicine

Introduction

Occupational contact dermatitis is the result of an inflammatory reaction in the skin to substances or materials with which people have contact in the course of their work. It occurs in almost every industry to some extent, but some jobs carry a higher risk than others perhaps because of processes directly involving damage to the skin or because substances toxic to the skin are used. Contact dermatitis is subdivided into two types, not for academic purposes but because the accurate diagnosis of the specific type determines the management of the condition and the likely outcome in terms of being able to continue in the same job.

The commoner type by far is irritant contact dermatitis which can develop in any individual who is exposed to enough of a physical or chemical skin irritant for a sufficiently long period. The onset may be sudden in the case of strong irritants such as concentrated acids or alkalis, or gradual over a period of time with weaker irritants such as cutting oils, detergents, soaps or repeated mechanical friction.

Less common, but usually more serious from the job retention point of view, is allergic contact dermatitis in which the skin becomes sensitised, or allergic, to specific substances (allergens). Once sensitisation has occurred it is irreversible and will result in increasingly severe reactions to smaller and smaller amounts of the allergen, necessitating complete elimination of contact. Common examples include chromates in cement, epoxy resins, acrylic resins, metals such as nickel, hardwoods, biocides and certain plants.

It is not possible to distinguish between the two types by clinical examination only. Patch testing is essential by a dermatologist with special expertise in occupational dermatitis.

How common is occupational contact dermatitis?

Estimates vary depending on the source of the information but the Health and Safety Executive quotes the possible loss of 4 million working days due to skin disorders generally, with a cost to industry of £20 million. The Labour Force Survey in 1990 indicated a possible 54,000 cases of skin disease caused by work and another 30,000 made worse. The EPI-DERM reporting scheme at the University of Manchester has assisted in identifying higher risk occupations and the commoner skin irritants and allergens.

Jobs identified as 'higher risk' include:

- chemical operatives and laboratory technicians;
- hairdressers and beauticians;
- machine tool operators/metal working fitters;
- florists;
- electroplaters;
- healthcare workers;
- chefs/cooks;
- cleaners;
- printers;
- textile workers;
- construction workers.

Common skin irritants and allergens include:

- rubbers;
- wet work;
- hairdressing chemicals;
- soaps;
- epoxy and other resins;
- plant saps;
- nickel;
- foods;
- petroleum oils;
- cutting oils and coolants;
- cement;
- biocides.

It is important to realise that high hazard jobs do not automatically carry a high risk of dermatitis occurring as, if the law is complied with in a practical sense with effective skin care policies and good working practices, the problem is almost entirely preventable.

What does the law require?

Six different sets of regulation have particular relevance to maintaining healthy skin at work and preventing occupational dermatitis. These are:

1. The Control of Substances Hazardous to Health Regulations 1994 (COSHH).
2. The Management of Health and Safety at Work Regulations 1992 (MHSR).
3. Workplace (Health, Safety and Welfare) Regulations 1992.
4. Personal Protective Equipment at Work Regulations 1992.
5. Chemicals (Hazard Information and Packaging) Regulations 1993 (CHIP).
6. Reporting of Injuries, Diseases and Dangerous Occurrences Regulations 1995.

In essence, the combined impact of compliance with the above regulations should result in:

- ready availability of information on chemical hazards;
- 'competent assistance' in evaluating risks (either inhouse or 'bought in');
- effective risk assessment in processes carried out and substances used;
- adequate controls where satisfactory, safer alternatives cannot be identified;
- regular and sensitive monitoring of the effectiveness of these controls;
- adequate and appropriate welfare facilities;
- provision of personal protective equipment which is suited to its purpose;
- health surveillance of employees identified as being at risk of dermatitis;
- reporting of cases of occupational dermatitis to HSE or the local authority.

What does an effective skin care policy consist of?

The skin is the boundary between humans and their environment. The horny outer layer acts as an extremely effective barrier to water passing outwards and toxic substances, including microorganisms, passing inwards – providing it is intact. Cuts, abrasions, pre-existing skin disease or dry patches make this barrier layer easier to penetrate, so that skin moisture is lost and inflammatory reactions result which can then lead on to occupational dermatitis. The skin becomes reddened, scaly, cracked and blistering with itchiness and severe discomfort and secondary bacterial infection is almost certain to occur.

Thus, the essential elements in an effective skin care policy should be geared to:

- appropriate pre-employment screening procedures to ensure that those with pre-existing skin disease are not put at additional and unacceptable risk (but not excluding everyone with a skin condition from jobs which involve minimal risk to the skin, as this would amount to unfair discrimination);
- education of the workforce on the risks of their job;
- maintaining the skin in good condition and avoiding contact with hazardous processes or materials (by substitution with safer alternatives, if possible);
- provision of personal protective equipment (PPE) as a last resort which is of a suitable design and material for the intended purpose;
- training of the users of PPE on selection, proper use and maintenance;
- provision of pre-work protection cream against the specific contaminant;
- a cleanser to remove the skin protection cream and the contaminant;
- adequate drying facilities for the numbers involved;
- an after work moisturer to replenish the barrier layer;
- instruction on reporting any abnormal skin signs promptly to a designated member of staff, in addition to regular surveillance for problems by a responsible person.

Costs of occupational contact dermatitis

Employers often voice the opinion that skin care is a personal matter and one for which they should not be expected to take responsibility. Obviously, skin care outside work is an individual's own business, but within the workplace people are required to carry out processes which may damage their skin, for example, handling sharp metal parts or exposure to hazardous chemicals such as solvents or naturally occurring substances such as the sap of plants. Modern health and safety legislation places the responsibility firmly on the employer's shoulders to ensure that unnecessary harm is not inflicted on people in the course of performing their duties. The individual still has personal responsibility to co-operate with the employer, carry out instructions and comply with provisions aimed at protecting their own health.

The costs of failing to take the necessary steps to ensure health maintenance are high:

- skilled staff with dermatitis being unable to work in their usual jobs, or at all;
- lost production or problems with quality assurance;
- cost of sickness absence in the short term and civil litigation eventually;
- increased insurance premiums;
- possible penalties by HSE for breaches of legislation;
- cost of recruiting and retraining of replacement staff;
- damage to staff morale, and industrial relations, for perceived neglect of employee well-being.

Although the implementation of an effective skin care policy involves some capital expenditure on the part of the employer, the benefits are substantial when compared to the possible costs of ignoring the legal and moral obligations to do so. A proactive approach is undoubtedly preferable to being forced to take action after problems have occurred.

Managing an outbreak of occupational dermatitis

All cases of occupational dermatitis must be treated on an individual basis and important decisions on change of job or dismissal on health grounds should be based on expert advice from a doctor with specialist knowledge of occupational skin disorders. Accurate diagnosis is vitally important so that guidance on future exposure can be based on objective evidence from, for example, patch testing. Changes to the work environment to remove or reduce risks should take precedence over removing people with problems. A trial resumption of duties in an improved environment is preferable to relocation or termination of employment.

Workplaces where there is a known high risk of dermatitis should have a stated policy for dealing with any problems arising, as job insecurity may deter reporting at an early stage before conditions become serious or irreversible.

Conclusion

The prevention of skin problems is possible with awareness, motivation and a logical approach to implementing legislation in a practical manner. The following sequence of questions may be helpful to the employer in this respect:

- Am I, or do I have staff, competent in risk assessment techniques?

- Could any of my work processes do physical harm to the skin of employees?
- Could I make changes to achieve the required results while reducing risks?
- Do I use any substances known to be harmful to the skin?
- Might research identify satisfactory but safer alternatives?
- Are my recruitment policies fair and appropriate?
- Are my staff adequately informed about risks and trained in use of controls?
- Do I have an adequate skin care policy in place and do staff know about it?
- Do the welfare facilities meet the needs of the staff using them?
- Is time allowed in work schedules for handwashing at breaks?
- If gloves have to be worn, are they suitable for the intended purpose?
- Do I have a policy for dealing fairly with people who develop dermatitis?

References

1 Hodgson, J T, Jones, J R, Elliott, R C and Osman J (1993) *Self-reported work-related illness*, HSE, Sudbury.
2 National Eczema Society, *Eczema at work – a practical guide for employers*, National Eczema Society, London.
3 HSE, *Health surveillance of occupational skin disease*, HSE Guidance Note MS24, HSE, Sudbury.
4 HSE, *Preventing dermatitis at work* – Advice for employers and employees, HSE leaflet.

PART FOUR

HEALTH PROMOTION

14

Workplace Health Promotion: Providing a Rationale

Helen Kogan

Sickness absence, according to a CBI survey[1], cost British industry some 175 million days in 1994. This figure is particularly stark when compared to a mere 278,000 days lost to industrial action in the same year. Translated to direct costs for UK business this equated to £10 billion, with further indirect costs of £6 billion. Respondents to the CBI survey felt that minor ailments such as colds accounted for the great majority of sickness, with stress and mental illness also high on the list. Increasingly companies looking to reduce their absenteeism rate have turned to proactive ways to improve the general health of the workforce. Exercise regimes, healthy eating choices in company canteens, smoking cessation groups and stress counselling have become strategies in the overall aim of promoting workplace health. But what proof is there that these measures actually improve the health of the employee, thereby reducing sickness absence, and should these activities be financed by industry?

Workplace wellness experience in the USA

The workplace wellness movement was first experienced in North America where companies, concerned with reducing their healthcare costs, began to examine ways to improve the general health of their employees. While evaluation of workplace health promotion programmes is still in its infancy in the UK there has been considerable work carried out in the USA to assess the outcome of such schemes.

A review of policies by the London Business School[2] examined companies and their research data to assess the impact of wellness schemes. The author, Neville Munroe, concluded that the benefits could be subdivided into two kinds: the first being pure health and well-being gains that participating employees enjoyed from healthier lifestyles; the second related to the productivity and absenteeism levels of these employees. Munroe points to perhaps the earliest and most comprehensive evaluation of a wellness programme undertaken in the USA by the pharmaceuticals giant Johnson & Johnson. Its 'Live for Life' programme was first piloted in 1978 and targeted a workforce of 30,000 employees in seven sites. The cost of the schemes per employee at the time was US$125.

Over the next ten years the programme was further developed and offered:

- a health profile;
- a three-hour lifestyle seminar;
- lifestyle improvement activities such as nutritional advice, exercise, weight loss and control, smoking cessation, stress management and other topics;
- incentives and facilities to encourage regular exercise and other aspects of healthy living.

Following evaluation of the scheme it was found that, among other health-related impacts, employees had increased both exercise tolerance and participation rates and there had been a 22.6 per cent success rate through smoking cessation programmes compared to the general population cessation rate of 5 per cent.

The economic impact was measured in terms of the decrease in healthcare costs for participating employees. Johnson & Johnson calculated that the annual return on investment was approximately 30 per cent although this did not take into account the financial benefits of reduced absenteeism and increased employee morale.

While the Johnson & Johnson results impressed many UK organisations looking to similar schemes, transposition of the results is still hard to achieve considering the different healthcare systems. Healthcare costs are still met by the tax payer in the UK rather than the system of private health insurance for which US employers are expected to pay for their employees. The incentives for a workplace wellness culture is therefore far greater in the USA. However, experience in the UK also suggests that there are benefits for companies considering such schemes. However, before examining British examples of workplace wellness experience it is important to look at some of the arguments and concerns that have been expressed as to whether such policies are needed at all and, if they are, what safeguards and evaluative processes should be put in place.

Rationale for workplace wellness programmes

Since the late 1980s British companies have also been looking at the possibility of improving their employees' health. Without the American incentive of reducing healthcare costs there has been a more ambiguous rationale for such schemes. Initially, many companies saw the 'feel good factor' as a return in itself. Companies believed that employees who felt that the company cared about their wellbeing were likely to be more productive and loyal in the long term. However, recent years have begun to see a more exacting justification for such schemes. Cost effectiveness, clear outcomes and whether or not such schemes are within the realm of organisational responsibility are all questions that are increasingly being asked before embarking on such policies. Indeed, there has been much debate as to the appropriateness of certain initiatives, such as breast cancer screening, when parallel programmes, run by the NHS, already exist. Furthermore, there has been an increasingly vocal debate by occupational health professionals as to whether or not this is an appropriate function for their departments when the primary concern must be to prevent ill health from workplace processes.

The concern for many has been that health promotion has become the predominant activity of occupational health professionals, with less time spent on preventing the causes of ill health derived from work practices. This argument, however, appears to hold little sway with employers who in a recent survey[3] declared that they wanted more health promotion to be carried out by occupational health nurses. A balance then is called for when looking at the potential for health promotion policies. Perhaps the first action should be an honest appraisal of occupational health policies and whether or not they are being fully resourced and implemented before any move to implement health promotion campaigns occurs.

A further argument has been forwarded that suggests that it is not appropriate for employers to focus solely on an individual's responsibility for his or her behaviour. The reasons behind an individual's health choices are multifactorial. Some twenty years ago the seminal Black Report looked at why individuals chose to take actions that affected their health and found that socio-economic causes were predominant influences. Companies looking at health promotion as a way to shape behaviour should therefore be aware of such influences and the limitations that are placed on individuals. Cox[4] argues for such an approach to be developed by organisations:

> Focusing solely on the individual's responsibility for his or her behaviour and health can result in a very narrow view of health promotion, and can distract from asking questions about the reasons why individuals behave in a healthy or unhealthy manner. If the

workplace does offer a convenient stage for acting out the theatre of health promotion, because it dominates much of the lives of most adults, then it is likely that it also plays a major influence in shaping their behaviour and in determining whether that behaviour is healthy or unhealthy. A sensible and comprehensive approach to the promotion of health must therefore ask questions about the factors that shape health-related behaviour, and seek to assess their influence.

Indeed, companies with mature wellness programmes have found that while there will always be a percentage of employees – the 'worried well' – who will take the opportunity to utilise fully the facilities provided, there is an equal number of those that health promotion messages still find hard to reach. The challenge for workplace wellness schemes, therefore, appears to be to try to involve those employees who are resistant to such messages. This takes us back full circle to the argument that health behaviour is affected by a complicated mix of social and economic factors – a crucial component for employers to understand before undertaking such schemes.

Consideration of these arguments has been an important element in whether or not those British companies that have implemented wellness schemes reap the benefits. Important too is the ability to set up proper evaluative procedures. This will not only demonstrate whether or not there is a cost benefit justification for a company to support such programmes but could also help create a research pool for other companies looking to initiate such schemes. A *Health of the Nation Workplace Task Force Report*[5] proposed a process of evaluation which is summarised in Box 14.1.

BOX 14.1
Summary of process of evaluation

- **Step 1**: Clarify aims and objectives of the proposed health promotion programme.
- **Step 2**: Design the framework of the revaluation and decide what questions you want to ask.
- **Step 3**: Design the framework for evaluation and decide how you are going to measure change.
- **Step 4**: Collect the data.
- **Step 5**: Evaluate the results to determine effectiveness of programme.
- **Step 6**: Make recommendations.

Organisations such as the Wellness Forum also provide guidance for companies interested in establishing such processes (address given in Appendix III).

Experience of British companies

British companies that have developed evaluation methods have released data[6] to argue the cost-benefits of workplace health promotion. These include:

- Don and Low Group – a range of health education programmes resulted in a 1.5 per cent reduction in its absenteeism rate.
- Whitbread PLC – implementation of an Employee Assistance Programme for stress counselling and a 'look after yourself' campaign which includes fitness facilities and no smoking policies has resulted in an estimated £3 return for every £1 invested in this programme.
- Ford Motor Company Ltd – extensive occupational health service is also backed by health promotion activities which include measuring general health, lifestyle, lung function and cardiac risk factors. The company reports a 20 per cent decrease in sickness and early retirement rates.

Examples of specific workplace wellness schemes are further demonstrated in this book. However, while the examples given above seem highly impressive it should be remembered that health promotion is not necessarily an easy way out to improve workforce performance efficiency and productivity. Organisational issues might be the cause of employee discontent and companies need to make an honest appraisal which takes the entire company structure into account. For example, stress counselling may prove helpful. However, if companies do not listen to their employees' concerns about management culture and structure, with a view to change, no improvements in absenteeism and staff turnover will be achieved. Health promotion is not a panacea for all ills and companies need to be prepared to take action when organisational issues become apparent as causes of employee ill health and absenteeism. It might well be that embarking on wellness programmes could be simply to open a 'can of worms' and companies must be committed to tackling such issues from the outset.

Reasonable expectations

Given that so many companies have expressed an interest in health promotion means that it is a policy that looks likely to remain and be developed even further in the future. However, companies that are initiating such programmes need to be clear about what they can reasonably expect, how to evaluate the outcomes and, most importantly, whether or not they have provided comprehensive and effective services to prevent ill health from workplace processes. Confident that these measures have been achieved, workplace health promotion can provide access to the 'working well' and may prevent the future onset of disease involving financial and human costs to the individual, employer and society as a whole.

References

1 CBI/Centre-file (1995) *Managing Absence*, London.
2 Munroe, N (1994), *Worksite Wellness: The Financial Justification of Corporate Health Promotion Schemes*, London Business School, unpublished research.
3 Ballard, J (1996) 'Occupational health nurses: an OHR survey', *Occupational Health Review*, January/February.
4 Cox, T, Griffiths, A, Kerr, J (1996) *Workplace Health: Employee Fitness and Exercise*, Taylor and Francis, London.
5 *Health of the Nation Workplace Task Force Report*, unpublished, September 1993.
6 CBI/BUPA (1993) *Working for your Health*, London.

15

Health Promotion Case Studies

Health Education Authority

Introduction

According to a survey carried out for the Health Education Authority (HEA) in the spring of 1995 almost two-thirds of businesses now acknowledge their responsibility to improve all aspects of the health and wellbeing of their workforce. The majority are also prepared to make an investment in workplace health promotion, with key benefits being seen as improved staff morale, reduced staff turnover and an improved image for the organisation. And, as the cost of sickness absence soars even more British companies are becoming interested in workplace health schemes.

Workplace absenteeism is now costing British business more than £27 million a day, with 175 million working days lost as a result (CBI, 1993). Failure to tackle this problem also has other financial implications, with a growing risk of litigation by staff suffering work-related illnesses such as stress and RSI (Repetitive Strain Injury). The introduction of new Statutory Sick Pay (SSP) legislation in 1994, abolishing the reimbursement of employers' SSP costs, is a further reason why companies are now giving a high priority to the health and wellbeing of all employees.

The HEA, as the nation's leading health promotion agency, has been playing a crucial role in encouraging the development of health programmes in the workplace. The HEA's team, based at Canterbury, launched a new Health at Work Awards Scheme in 1995, setting a national benchmark for quality standards in workplace health promotion.

Employers stand to gain as much from workplace health promotion schemes as their employees and investment in these schemes should be seen as a sound business decision. Health is not an optional extra in business – and the saying that prevention is better than cure has never been more true.

While individual lifestyles such as smoking or excessive drinking may not be obvious health at work issues, they may still affect an employee's productivity. It is therefore in the interests of employers to promote improvements in their employees both inside and outside the workplace.

The HEA has received testimonials from companies of all sizes, in the public and private sectors, which clearly show that health at work programmes do have a beneficial impact throughout organisations.'

The Health at Work Award scheme is intended to encourage and acknowledge the efforts of all employers with a permanent commitment to improving staff health and the working environment. Three separate categories of Award are available:

Category 1: emphasises the need for planning, awareness raising and consultation.

Category 2: includes all of Category 1 and focuses on the development of management practices and monitoring systems.

Category 3: encompasses all of the above and emphasises organisational development issues.

The Award is designed for organisations at different stages and allows them to respond to their own organisation's health at work needs. All of the categories are open to organisations of any size.

The five case studies featured in this handbook have been supplied by employers firmly committed to a structured workplace health promotion strategy.

C&A Case Study: Smoking

Background

C&A is a multi-sited leading fashion retailer with high street retail outlets throughout the UK. Its headquarters is in London and has a co-ordinating role for their health promotion programme.

In an attempt gradually to phase in a smoking policy, C&A called upon the services of Health at Work. A questionnaire was sent to all staff to elicit their views on the policy. The outcome of this was that both smokers and non-smokers were happy to work towards the phased introduction of a smoking policy. The strategy that they developed had three phases which took place over one year:

- **Phase 1.** Smoking facilities offered between 10 am and 4 pm only.
- **Phase 2.** Smoking permitted between 12 noon and 2 pm.
- **Phase 3.** Implementation of policy and a total ban on smoking in any of the buildings.

Health at Work was invited in prior to Phase 1 to assist those who expressed a need for help in giving up smoking. A number of Health at Work consultants with relevant expertise attended a training course on tailoring their 'smoke stop' programme specifically to the needs of C&A. These consultants subsequently ran 'smoke stop' courses at various central locations throughout the UK. Having attended a four-week course, participants were recalled one month later to monitor their progress.

Outcomes

In addition to the following outcomes, the procedures adopted by C&A serve as a model of good practice when introducing and implementing a workplace health policy.

- Created a healthier environment.
- Cleaner working environment.
- The structured manner in which this issue was tackled created a more positive attitude within the workforce.
- This initiative was a starting-point from which the company began to look at a corporate health strategy. C&A are currently working towards an alcohol policy and their plans for 1996 encompassed a variety of other health issues.

TESTIMONIAL

The experience and expertise of the Health at Work team greatly helped with the smooth implementation of our smoking policy. Their flexible approach enabled us to put together a tailor-made programme for our staff.

Tricia Thorne
Senior Personnel Officer
October 1995

TSB Case Study: Stress

Background

The TSB plc headquarters in London has approximately 500 employees and the work they carry out relates to the transmission of money across the banking network via paper (cheques) and electronic transfer. The nature of this work is sedentary and repetitive and in some cases, involves shiftwork. The TSB has existing policies on both smoking and alcohol.

Approximately two years ago Health at Work was invited to help develop its health promotion programme in the field of stress management. This initiative was taken in order to support staff during a period of ongoing organisational change. It was also hoped that this would help reduce the level of absenteeism which may have been stress related.

After negotiation it was decided to run a number of workshops for all staff (senior management to junior clerical) including sessions run during the night shifts. The aim of these one-day workshops was to give the participants an opportunity to identify their personal stressors and stress reactions. Staff were then given the opportunity to try out a range of practical coping skills and stress management techniques. This enabled them to identify the skills/techniques most appropriate to their individual needs. Participants were given an information pack which included material from 'Positive Stress at Work'.

Outcomes

Pre and post evaluations took place to monitor the effectiveness of the workshops. The outcomes were as follows:

- There was a 13 per cent increase in knowledge related to stress. The significance of this is that a base line knowledge of stress is a key factor to stress management.
- There was a general improvement in personal assertiveness and decision-making ability which has helped improve communication channels.
- There was a 10 per cent increase in numbers of staff exercising regularly as a means of coping with stress. This is a very positive outcome since the benefits of exercise extend further than stress management in improving overall good health and wellbeing.
- In relation to above, TSB saw a reduction in absenteeism.
- Staff more motivated. There was a more positive view of the organisation because this was not a 'technical work-related course' but a practical workshop to help the individual.

TESTIMONIAL

Helping staff understand their own stress levels and tolerances and giving them the tools to deal with stress themselves should produce long-term benefits to the organisation.

Gill Bland
Personnel Manager
October 1995

Post Office Case Study: Healthy Eating

The Post Office Occupational Health Service provides advice to over 180,000 employees throughout the UK. With experience of a pro-active health promotion established over a number of years it has been found that 'tailored information' which has been especially written or adapted for use within the Post Office is effective in communicating health messages.

As part of an overall approach to encouraging healthy eating a need was established to support excellent inhouse catering initiatives led by Quadrant, with high quality information and advice.

Although it was clear that many recipe books have been published and many leaflets exist on the subject of healthy eating, a small team of occupational health nurses developed an innovative approach in this area.

The team invited recipe suggestions from colleagues throughout Britain. Their overall approach was to seek suggestions for genuine 'good eating' following basic principles to encourage fibre, fruit and vegetable eating and to reduce intake of salt, sugar and fat. It sought to underline the importance of eating a balanced diet and to provide information in an attractive easily read format.

The results of their labours was *The Light Hearted Cookbook*, a collection of delicious, tried and tested recipes, supported by some very basic information regarding healthy eating and the importance of a balanced diet.

The working group quickly collected an interesting collection of recipes which varied from simple sauces and starters through to exciting suggestions such as brown bread ice cream. The final selection was published in a paperback book which has been widely used to support health promotion initiatives within the Post Office.

The book has been equally useful both in providing information to those seeking advice for health problems and as a prize to encourage participation in competitions and events.

While it was certainly possible to take a similar book 'off the shelf', producing our own literature of this type has proved popular and effective.

LDDC Case Study: Physical Activity

The London Docklands Development Corporation (LDDC) is a non-departmental public body established in 1981 to manage the development and regeneration of derelict land within the London docks. Following completion of its task the LDDC will cease operations in March 1998. Staffing levels have decreased from 500 to 200 over the past six years. A progressive programme of redundancy will continue to the point of dissolution.

LDDC has been pro-active in promoting health throughout the organisation and has succeeded in developing an innovative and positive programme of activities and services for staff and consultants at relatively little cost to the Corporation. The programme operates under the name of 'OUTLOOK – LDDC working for a healthier future'. The programme has been developed by LDDC human resource team in collaboration with health and fitness consultants.

The physical activity element of the programme has been consistently pro-active since the signing of the Look After Your Heart Workplace Charter in May 1989.

LDDC relocated to its current building in July 1990. This provided the opportunity to install a small gymnasium. Employees and long-term consultants were encouraged through the inhouse magazine to take a more active approach to their health. LDDC contracted professional health and fitness consultants to advise on the selection and installation of equipment as well as devise a management programme to ensure the safe and effective use of the gym.

As a result of this collaboration LDDC continues to promote

physical activity and exercise at work, and offer the following wide range of services to staff and consultants:

- gymnasium;
- personal health assessments;
- personal fitness programmes;
- customised computer analysis of individual progress;
- monthly statistical reports;
- weekly aerobic exercise class;
- weekly yoga class;
- blood pressure monitoring;
- outdoor activity weekends;
- general lifestyle advice;
- home-based exercise programmes for the non-gym user;
- alternative therapy sessions, reflexology, aromatherapy, holistic massage.

Outcomes

It could be argued that the physical activity and exercise initiative has greatly contributed to the following:

- Low absenteeism. Figures for 1995–6 – 2.84 per cent which compares to a public sector average of 5.5 per cent (Apac National HR Database 1995).
- Low occupational disease and illness. No reportable accidents and very few work-related illnesses. Reports made to the board level Safety Audit Committee every quarter.
- Levels of participation. Regular attendances to exercise and yoga classes. High gym usage. Increasing number of one-to-one consultations with the health and fitness consultants. High attendance to other training and health options. Increased participation in charitable events, London Marathon, Dragon Boat racing (MIND).
- Citizens Charter targets met annually.
- High staff satisfaction with the diversity of opportunities for increased physical activity provided by the Corporation.

TESTIMONIAL

The initial signing of the LAYH Workplace Charter and the creation of the gymnasium has provided a focus for a wider health and wellness programme. The LDDC has acknowledged national and international research and recommendations, focusing on the health gains derived from increased physical activity from both an individual and organisational basis.

Staff are encouraged and supported to use flexitime and free 'health time' to become more physically active. In terms of motivation, productivity and morale this is a very good investment. Health is an important (vital) part of our overall human resources strategy for effective 'wind down' of operations.

David Lowman
Head of Personnel & Administration

NMUK Case Study: Men's Health – Testicular Self-examination

Health promotion provides the opportunity to empower the masses and enable individuals to lead more worthwhile and positive lives. The workplace has been shown to be a suitable arena for such health promotion initiatives.

This is a brief history of the experience of the industrial and organisation health occupational health team based at Nissan Motor Manufacturing (UK) Limited (NMUK) in devising and presenting a series of health promotion sessions.

Initially, market research was completed to identify the needs of the workforce, looking at age, gender, existing knowledge levels and awareness of health-related issues. From this, a selection of topics was chosen.

Following extensive research, a series of health promotion packages were designed which would effectively complement the set criteria (i.e. short, sharp, interactive sessions that appealed to all intellectual levels). An element of adaptability was incorporated, allowing each session to be equally effective no matter what the teaching environment, from lecture theatre to workshop rest area. All nursing staff have formal teaching qualifications and are equally competent to deliver any of the health promotion sessions on demand. This allowed flexibility in the day-to-day management and staffing of the occupational health department. In financial terms, the cost of producing the health promotion packages was minimal.

The senior nursing officer from the medical centre was invited to give a presentation to publicise the health promotion initiative to the directors and managers of NMUK. The uptake was phenomenal; within three weeks the diary for 1996 was fully booked.

The topic, testicular self-examination, was particularly well received, and accounted for 37 per cent of the total number of 202 sessions. During the testicular self-examination sessions a number of varied teaching strategies was utilised, including the use of a video to demonstrate testicular self-examination. The occupational health nurses also designed and published a series of humorous leaflets and visual teaching aids.

Outcomes

The main objectives were to raise awareness of the topic, to enable the individual to self-examine and to highlight the significance of early diagnosis. Initially the topic of testicular self-examination fuelled schoolboy innuendos and humour. However, the significant increase in numbers of people attending the medical centre for advice after finding a testicular abnormality suggests that the barrier of embarrassment has been effectively broken down. They now appear to have a new confident approach and accept responsibility for their own health, each worker realising that he is as susceptible as the next man.

During the evaluation of the campaign one of the positive but rather unexpected outcomes identified was that nursing teamwork, job satisfaction and motivation was clearly raised and will carry on into the promotion of health in 1997.

Our primary objective was to identify those at risk. We would suggest that this is demonstrated by the following case study.

Men's health: testicular self-examination

Checklist material

- Market research re client group.
- Availability of relevant, up-to-date literature.
- Availability of distributable materials.
- Cost of materials, i.e. leaflets.
- Availability of staff to deliver talk.
- Availability of teaching aids, i.e. video.
- Suitability of leaflets.
- Lesson plan, agreeable to all staff.

Legal requirements

- Confidentiality.
- To meet with Health and Safety Executive legislation and guidance.
- To promote the use of appropriate personal protective equipment.
- Liaise with outside agencies.

CASE STUDY

A 25-year-old skilled production line worker attended the medical centre and quietly asked to speak to 'the nurse who gave the talk yesterday'. This man, a father of two, had found a testicular lump. Following discussion with the nurse it was agreed that he should consult his GP. He was subsequently referred to a surgeon for investigation, then surgery. The occupational health department staff provided reassurance during this stressful period.

We suggest that this alone justifies the health promotion campaign on moral and economic grounds, returning a highly skilled man back to good health and productive employment.

Occupational Health Nursing Staff
NMUK
November 1996

The Nursing Officers Occupational Health Department NMUK wish to thank the contributors for their prompt and generous input into our health promotion project – Testicular Self-Examination. From the information provided we were able to design and produce our own health promotion teaching package.

References

Austoker, Joan (1994) 'Cancer prevention in primary care – screening for ovarian, prostatic and testicular cancers', *BMJ*, 308:315–20.

Bonnar, Irene and Gordon, Kay (1991) 'Testicular self-examination: 2' *Occupational Health*, March:87–8.

Bonnar, Irene and Gordon, Kay (1991) 'Testicular cancer – case studies', *Occupational Health*, July:208–9.

Carlin, Pamela J (1996) 'Testicular self-examination: a public awareness program', *Public Health Reports*, January–February, 1(1):98–102.

Hawkes, Helen (1993) *One Lump Too Many*, supplement to *Company* magazine, February:15–17. In association with the Health Education Authority.

Hobbs, Andrew (1995) 'Ging, gang, goolie goolie ...' *Healthlines*, July–August:7.

Moller, Henrik, *et al.* (1994) 'Risk of testicular cancer after vasectomy: cohort study of over 73,000 men', *BMJ*, 309:295–9.

Moul, Judd W, *et al.* (1990) 'Delay in diagnosis and survival in testicular cancer: impact of effective therapy and changes during 18 years', *The Journal of Urology*, 143:520–23.

Sharpe, Richard M and Skakkebaek, Niels E (1993) 'Are oestrogens involved in falling sperm counts and disorders of the male reproductive tract?', *The Lancet*, 341:1392–5.

Summers, Elizabeth (1995) 'Vital signs', *Nursing Times*, 91(25):46–7.

Thornhill, John A, *et al.* (1986) 'Recent trends in mortality due to testicular cancer in Ireland: a comparison with England and Wales', *Journal of Epidemiology and Community Health*, 40:218–22.

PART FIVE

APPENDICES

Appendix I: Sources of Information on Work-related Ill Health*

Population surveys

- Population surveys of self-reported conditions are a major source of information. In 1990 people sampled in the Labour Force Survey (LFS) were asked: 'In the past 12 months, have you suffered from any illness, disability or other physical problem that was caused or made worse by your work? Please include any work you have done in the past.'
- Those who answered affirmatively were asked further questions about the nature of the illness and the job that was thought to have given rise to it. While not all self-reports of illness can be taken at face value, it is of some interest, in its own right, to know what workers think about the cause of their illnesses, and the validity of the responses was examined in various ways, using both internal evidence and comparison with other sources of statistics. Where other statistics were available for comparison, LFS estimates were of a consistent order of magnitude, allowing for differences of coverage of the other sources. A full assessment of the reliability of self-reports of different types of work-related illness is given in the detailed report of the survey[1].
- A further survey is currently under way, with refinements and additions to the earlier methods including the seeking of confirmation and additional details from the doctors of people who report conditions. It is planned that the results will be published in 1997.

---

*Appendix material supplied by the Health and Safety Executive.

Industrial injuries

- Under the Industrial Injuries Scheme, compensation may be payable for occupational diseases which appear on the list of prescribed diseases. The Industrial Injuries Advisory Council (IIAC) provides the government with independent advice on the prescription of diseases and on the operation of the scheme. Diseases are only prescribed where there is a well-established link with specific occupational causes and where it is possible to frame terms of prescription such that the majority of cases which meet the medical and occupational requirements will be genuine cases of occupational disease. Annual numbers of cases may be influenced by factors that affect sufferers' propensity to make a claim, such as awareness of the scheme. For most prescribed diseases, disability must be assessed at 14 per cent or more for benefit to be payable, but the statistics in Chapter 9, Table 9.5 include all those assessed at 1 per cent or more. (For deafness, figures are only available for those assessed at 20 per cent or more disability.)

Voluntary reporting schemes

- There are voluntary schemes, co-ordinated by academic medical units with HSE funding, in which participating specialist doctors and occupational physicians report new cases of diseases that they believe to be attributable to the patient's work. These schemes comprise SWORD (Surveillance of Occupational and Work-related Respiratory Disease, co-ordinated by the National Heart and Lung Institute), and EPI-DERM (co-ordinated by the University of Manchester Centre for Occupational Health) which, as its name implies, deals with skin diseases. Other kinds of occupational and work-related diseases, including musculoskeletal disorders and deafness, are currently being reported under an experimental pilot scheme.
- Coverage of the voluntary schemes is limited by the fact that not all cases will be seen by a participating doctor. In general it is the more serious cases that are likely to be seen by a chest physician or dermatologist, while access to occupational physicians varies according to individuals' type of work and their employers. The interpretation of trends may be complicated by the fact that the levels of voluntary participation may vary slightly from one year to the next. The 1995 SWORD figures in particular are known to have been affected by low participation rates. Fuller statistical breakdowns (including analyses by causative agent for asthma and dermatitis cases) are given in Health and Safety Statistics, and in reports by the SWORD co-ordinators in medical journals.[2]

Death certificates

- Death certificates are useful for monitoring fatal cases of diseases caused by asbestos, and certain other occupational lung diseases. They do not specifically identify mortality from all kinds of work-related ill health.

RIDDOR

- Injuries caused by chemicals at work, such as acute poisonings, burns, scalds, and gassings, are reportable under RIDDOR (Reporting of Injuries, Diseases and Dangerous Occurrences Regulations 1995) as industrial injuries if they cause more than three days unfitness for work (or are 'major' or fatal injuries). There is however substantial incompleteness of reporting of such incidents, and the information given does not always distinguish chemical injuries from the bulk of reported incidents which involve mechanical trauma. The figures given earlier in this chapter refer to reported injuries, where the coding indicates exposure to a harmful substance, or asphyxiation (but not drowning). Certain specified industrial diseases are also reportable under RIDDOR if the affected person is currently employed in the causative occupation and if the employer has received a doctor's diagnosis in writing.

1 Hodgson J T, Jones J R, Elliot R C, Osman J (1993) Self-reported work-related illness, HSE Research Paper 33, HSE Books, Sudbury.
2 Ross, D J, Sallie, B A and McDonald, J C (1995) 'SWORD '94: Surveillance of work-related and occupational respiratory disease in the UK', *Occupational Medicine*, **45**: 175–8.

Appendix II: Government Departments

Department of Health
Richmond House
79 Whitehall
London SW1A 2NS
Tel: 0171 210 3000
Fax: 0171 210 5523

Department of the Environment
Romney House
43 Marsham Street
London SW1P 2PY
Tel: 0171 276 0900

Health & Safety Commission
Rose Court
2 Southwark Bridge
London SE1 9HS
Tel: 0171 717 6630
Fax: 0171 717 6644

Health & Safety Executive
Directorate of Information & Advisory Services
St Hughs House
Stanley Precinct
Bootle
Merseyside L20 3QY
Tel: 0151 951 4000
Fax: 0151 951 4446
http://www.open.gov.uk/hse/hsehome.htm

Occupational Medicine & Hygiene Laboratory HSE
Broad Lane
Sheffield S3 7HQ

Her Majesty's Factory Inspectorate
Maritime House
1 Linten Road
Barking
Essex IJ11 8HF
Tel: 0181 235 8000
Fax: 0181 235 8080

Incomes Data Sevices Ltd
193 St John Street
London EC1V 4LS
Tel: 0171 250 3434
Fax: 0171 608 0949

Office of Population Censuses & Surveys
St Catherines House
10 Kingsway
London WC2B 6JP
Tel: 0171 242 0262

Health & Safety Executive Offices

Rose Court
2 Southwark Bridge
London SE1 9HS
Tel: 0171 717 6000
Fax: 0171 714 6717

St Hughs House
Stanley Precinct
Bootle
Merseyside L20 3QY
Tel: 0151 951 4000
Fax: 0151 922 5394

HSE Books
PO Box 1999
Sudbury
Suffolk CO10 6FS
Tel: 01787 881165
Fax: 01787 313995

HSE Information Services
Health & Safety Laboratory
Broad Lane
Sheffield S3 7HQ
Tel: 0541 545500
Fax: 0114 289 2333

Wales & West Regional Offices
(Covering; Avon, Cornwall, Devon, Gloucester, Somerset, Isles of Scilly,Clwyd, Dyfed, Gwent, Gwynedd, Mid Glamorgan, Powys, South Glamorgan, West Glamorgan, Hereford, Worcester, Shropshire & Staffordshire)

Brunel House
Fitzalan Road
Cardiff CF2 1SH
Tel: 01222 263 000
Fax: 01222 263 120

Inner City House
Mitchell Lane
Victoria Street
Bristol BS1 6AN
Tel: 0117 988 6000
Fax: 0117 926 2998

The Marches House
Midway
Newcastle-under-Lyme
Staffordshire ST5 1DT
Tel: 01782 602 300
Fax: 01782 602 400

Home Counties Regional Offices
(Covering; Bekshire, Dorset, Hampshire, Isle of Wight, Wiltshire, Essex, Norfolk, Suffolk, Bedfordshire, Cambridgeshire & Hertfordshire)

14 Cardiff Road
Luton LU1 1PP
Tel: 01582 444 200
Fax: 01582 444 320

Priestley House
Priestly Road
Basingstoke
Hants RG24 9NW
Tel: 01256 404 000
Fax: 01256 404 100

39 Baddow Road
Chelmsford
Essex CM2 0HL
Tel: 01245 706 200
Fax: 01245 706 222

London & South East Regional Offices
(Covering; all London Boroughs, Kent, Surrey, East Sussex & West Sussex)

1 Long Lane
Southwark
London SE1 4PG
Tel: 0171 556 2100
Fax: 0171 556 2200

Maritime House
1 Linton Road
Barking
Essex IG11 8HF
Tel: 0181 235 8000
Fax: 0181 235 8001

3 East Grinstead House
London Road
East Grinstead
West Sussex RH19 1RR
Tel: 01342 334 200
Fax: 01342 334 222

Midlands Regional Offices
(Covering, Leicestershire, Northamptonshire, Oxfordshire, Warwickshire, West Midlands, Derbyshire, Lincolnshire & Nottinghamshire)

McClaren Building
35 Dale End
Birmingham B4 7NP
Tel: 0121 607 6200
Fax: 0121 607 6349

5th Floor
Belgrave House
1 Greyfriars
Northampton NN1 2LQ
Tel: 01604 738 300
Fax: 01604 738 333

The Pearson Building
55 Upper Parliment Street
Nottingham NG1 6AU
Tel: 0115 9 712 800
Fax: 0115 9 712 802

Yorkshire & North East Regional Offices
(Covering; Humberside, South Yorkshire, North Yorkshire, West Yorkshire, Cleveland, Durham, Northumberland & Tyne & Wear)

Woodside House
261 Low House
Horsforth
Leeds LS18 5TW
Tel: 0113 283 4200
Fax: 0113 258 8029

Sovereign House
110 Queen Street
Sheffield S1 2ES
Tel: 0114 291 2300
Fax: 0114 291 2379

8 St Pauls Street
Leeds LS1 2LE
Tel: 0113 283 4200
Fax: 0113 283 4296

North West Regional Offices
(Covering; Greater Manchester, Cheshire, Merseyside, Cumbria & Lancashire)

The Triad
Stanley Road
Bootle
Merseyside L20 3PG
Tel: 0151 479 2200
Fax: 0151 479 2201

Quay House
Quay Street
Manchester M3 3JB
Tel: 0161 952 8200
Fax: 0161 952 8222

Victoria House
Ormskirk Road
Preston PR1 1HH
Tel: 01772 836 200
Fax: 01772 836 222

Scotland Offices
(Covering; Borders, Central, Fife, Grampian, Highland, Lothian, Tayside, Orkney Island, Shetland Island, Dumfries, Galloway, Strathclyde & the Western Isles)

Belford House
59 Belford Road
Edinburgh EH4 3UE
Tel: 0131 247 2000
Fax: 0131 247 2121

375 West George Street
Glasgow G2 4LW
Tel: 0141 275 3000
Fax: 0141 275 3001

Source: Health & Safety Executive, Merseyside

Appendix III: Sources of Advice

ACAS (Advisory, Consilliation & Arbitration Council)
Clifton House
83 Euston Road
London NW1 2RB
Tel: 0171 396 5100
Fax: 0171 396 5159

Accident Line
The Law Society
50 Chancery Lane
London WC2A 1SX
Tel: Freephone 0500 192939

Action on Smoking & Health
5–11 Mortimer Street
London W1N 7RH
Tel: 0171 637 9843
Fax: 0171 222 4343

AIRMIC – The Association of Insurance & Risk Managers
6 Lloyds Avenue
London EC3N 3AX
Tel: 0171 480 7610
Fax: 0171 702 3752

Alcohol Concern
305 Grays Inn Road
London WC1X 8QF
Tel: 0171 833 3471

Association of British Insurers
51 Gresham Street
London EC2V 7HQ
Tel: 0171 600 3333
Fax: 0171 696 8999

Association of Community Health Councils
30 Drayton Park
London N5 1PB
Tel: 0171 609 8405
Fax: 0171 700 1152

Association of Counselling at Work
c/o 1 Regent Place
Rugby
Warwickshire CV21 2PJ

Association of Noise Consultants
6 Trap Road
Guilden Morden
Near Royston
Herts SG8 0GE
Tel: 01763 852958
Fax: 01763 853251

Aston University Health & Safety Unit
Department of Mechanical & Production Engineering

Aston Triangle
Birmingham B4 7ET
Tel: 0121 359 3611
Fax: 0121 333 6350

Behavioural Science Consultants
c/o Professor HR Beech
Priory Hospital
Rappax Road
Hale
Atrincham
Cheshire WA15 0NX
Tel: 0161 904 0050
Fax: 0161 980 4322

British Heart Foundation
102 Gloucester Place
London W1H 4DH
Tel: 0171 935 0185
Fax: 0171 486 5820

British Medical Association
Tavistock Square
London WC1H 9JR
Tel: 0171 387 4499
Fax: 0171 383 6400

British Occupational Hygiene Society
Suite 2, Georgian House
Great Northern Road
Derby DE1 1LT
Tel: 01332 298101
Fax: 01332 298099

British Safety Council
National Safety Centre
Chancellors Road
London W6 9RS
Tel: 0181 741 1231
Fax: 0181 741 4555

British Standards Institution
389 Chiswick High Road
London W4 4AL
Tel: 0181 996 9000
Fax: 0181 996 7400

Cambridge University UK Public Health Page
Institute of Public Health
University Forvie Site
Robinson Way
Cambridge
Tel: 01223 330354
Fax: 01223 330168

Cancer Research Campaign
2 Carlton House Terrace
London SW1Y 5AR
Tel: 0171 224 1333
Fax: 0171 487 4310

CBI (Confederation British Industry)
103 Centre Point New Oxford Street
London WC1A
Tel: 0171 379 7400
Fax: 0171 240 1578

Central Toxicology Research Laboratory ICI Ltd
Alderley Park
Macclesfield
Cheshire SK10 4TJ
Tel: 01625 582332
Fax: 01625 582897

Centre for Health Economics
University of York
Heslington
York YO1 5DD
Tel: 01904 430000
Fax: 01904 433433

Chartered Institute of Enviromental Health
15 Hartfields
London SE1 8DJ
Tel: 0171 928 6006
Fax: 0171 827 5866

Council for Professions
Park House
184 Kennington Park Road
London SE11 4BI

Tel: 0171 582 0866
Fax: 0171 820 9684

EPI-DERM Occupational Skin Surveillance Scheme
Centre for Occupational Health
University of Manchester
Manchester M13 9PT
Tel: 0161 275 7103
Fax: 0161 275 5595

Ergonomics Society
Devonshire House
Devonshire Square
Loughborough
Leicestershire
LE11 3DW
Tel: 01509 234904
Fax: 01509 234904

Faculty of Occupational Medicine
Royal College of Physicians
6 St Andrews Place
London NW1 4LE
Tel: 0171 935 1174
Fax: 0171 487 5218

Health Education Authority
Hamilton House
Mabledon Place
London WC1H 9TX
Tel: 0171 383 3833
Fax: 0171 413 1843

Health & Safety Advice Centre
Unit 304
Argent Centre
60 Frederick Street
Birmingham B1 3HS
Tel: 0121 236 0801
Fax: 0121 236 3629

Imperial Cancer Research Fund
PO Box 123
Lincolns Inn Fields
London WC21 3PX
Tel: 0171 242 0200
Fax: 0171 269 3100

Industrial Injuries Advisory Council
A4 6th Floor
The Aldelphi
1 – 11 John Adam Street
London WC2N 6HT
Tel: 0171 962 8066
Fax: 0171 962 8004

The Industrial Society
Hyde House
48 Bryanstone Square
London W1H 7LN
Tel: 0171 262 2401
Fax: 0171 723 2007

The Industrial Society
Quadrant Court
49 Calthorpe Road
Edgbaston
Birmingham B15 2TT
Tel: 0121 454 6769
Fax: 0121 456 2715

Institute of Business Ethics
12 Palace Street
London SW1 5JA
Tel: 0171 931 0495
Fax: 0171 821 5819

Institute of Occupational Health
University of Birmingham
Edgbaston
Birmingham B15 2TT
Tel: 0121 414 3344
Fax: 0121 414 6217

Institute of Personnel Management
IPM House
35 Camp Road
London SW19 4UW
Tel: 0181 971 9000
Fax: 0181 263 3333

Institute of Radiation Protection
64 Dalkeith Road
Harpenden

Herts AL5 5PW
Tel: 01582 715026

Institute of Risk Management
Lloyds Avenue House
6 Lloyds Avenue
London EC3N 3AX
Tel: 0171 709 9808
Fax: 0171 709 0716

Institute of Trading Standards Administration
3 – 5 Hadleigh Business Centre
351 London Road
Hadleigh
Essex SS7 2BT
Tel: 01702 559 922
Fax: 01702 551161

Institution of Fire Engineers
148 New Walk
Leicester LE1 7QB
Tel: 0116 255 3654
Fax: 0116 247 1231

Institution of Occupational Safety & Health
The Grange
Highfield Drive
Wigston
Leicester LE18 1NN
Tel: 0116 257 1399
Fax: 0116 257 1451

International Stress Management Association UK
South Bank University LPSS
103 Borough Road
London SE1 0AA
Tel: 01702 584 025
Fax: 01702 584 025

Lawyers for Your Business
The Law Society
50 Chancery Lane
London WC2A 1SX
Tel: 0171 405 9075

The London Heart Clinic
22 Upper Wimpole Street
London W1M 7TA
Tel: 0171 486 8961
Fax: 0171 486 7918

London Hazards Centre Ltd
Interchange Studios
Dalby Street
London NW5 3NQ
Tel: 0171 267 3387
Fax: 0171 267 3397

Loss Prevention Council
Melrose Avenue
Borehamwood
Herts WD6 2BJ
Tel: 0181 207 2345
Fax: 0181 207 6305

Manchester Metropolitan University
Faculty of Community Studies, Law & Education
School of Law
Elizabeth Gaskell Campus
Hathersage Road
Manchester M13 0JA
Tel: 0161 247 2000
Fax: 0161 247 6309

Medical Research Council
20 Park Crescent
London W1N 4AL
Tel: 0171 636 5422
Fax: 0171 436 6179

National Back Pain Association
The Old Block Office
Elmtree Road
Teddington
Middlesex TW11 8ST
Tel: 0181 977 5474
Fax: 0181 943 5318

National Eczema Society
163 Eversholt Street
London NW1 1BU

Tel: 0171 388 4097
Fax: 0171 388 5882

NHS Confederation (Formerly NAHAT)
26 Chapter Street
London SW1P 4ND
Tel: 0171 233 7388
Fax: 0171 233 7390

Occupational & Enviromental Diseases Association
Mitre House
66 Abbey Road
Bush Hill Park
Enfield
Middlesex EN1 2HQ
Tel: 0181 360 8490

Office of Health Economics
12 Whitehall
London SW1A 2DY
Tel: 0171 930 9203
Fax: 0171 747 1419

Public Concern at Work
42 Kingsway
London WC2B 6BR
Tel: 0171 404 6609
Fax: 0171 404 6576

Quit
Victory House
170 Tottenham Court Road
London W1P 0HA
Tel: 0171 388 5775
Fax: 0171 388 5995

Repetitive Strain Injury Association
Chapel House
152 – 156 High Street
Yiewsley
West Drayton
Middlesex UB7 7BE
Tel: 01895 431134
Fax: 01895 431134

Robens Institute
University of Surrey
Guildford
Surrey GU2 5XH
Tel: 01483 568637
Fax: 01483 300803

RoSPA (The Royal Society for the Prevention of Accidents)
Cannon House
The Priory Queensway
Birmingham B4 6BS
Tel: 0121 248 2000
Fax: 0121 248 2001

Royal Brompton Hospital
Sydney Street
London SW3 6NP
Tel: 0171 352 8121
Fax: 0171 351 8473

Royal College of Physicians
11 St Andrews Place
Regents Park
London NW1 4LE
Tel: 0171 935 1174
Fax: 0171 487 5218

Royal College of Psychiatrists
17 Belgrave Square
London SW1X 8PG
Tel: 0171 235 2351
Fax: 0171 245 1231

The Royal Enviromental Health Institute of Scotland
3 Manor Place
Edinburgh
Tel: 0131 225 6999
Fax: 0131 225 3993

Royal Society of Medicine Services Ltd
1 Wimpole Street
London W1M 8AE
Tel: 0171 408 2119

Royal Society of Health
38A St Georges Drive
London SW1V 4BH
Tel: 0171 630 0121
Fax: 0171 976 6847

Safety Assessment Federation Ltd
Nutmeg House
60 Gainsford Street
Butlers Wharf
London SE1 2NY
Tel: 0171 403 0987
Fax: 0171 403 0137

Society of Occupational Medicine
6 St Andrews Place
London NW1 4LE
Tel: 0171 486 2641
Fax: 0171 486 0028

Standing Committee on Structural Safety
11 Upper Belgrave Street
London SW1X 8BH
Tel: 0171 235 4535
Fax: 0171 235 4294

Stress At Work
14 Albion Place
Northampton NN1 1UD
Tel: 01604 259 770

Sunderland Health Promotion Resources
North Sands Business Centre
Liberty Way
Sunderland SR6 0QA
Tel: 0191 514 2823
Fax: 0191 565 6433

Testicular Self-Examination – Video McCormack Ltd
Church House
Church Square
Leighton Buzzard
Bedfordshire LU7 7AE
Tel: 01525 851313
Fax: 01525 851314

TUC (Trades Union Congress)
Congress House
23 Great Russell Street
London WC1B 3LS
Tel: 0171 636 4030
Fax: 0171 636 0632

University of Manchester, Centre for Occupational Health
Medical School
Stopford Building
Oxford Road
Manchester M13 9PT
Tel: 0161 275 2000
Fax: 0161 200 4019

University of Newcastle
Division of Enviromental & Occupational Medicine
Medical School
School of Health Care Sciences
Framlington Place
Newcastle upon Tyne NE2 4HH
Tel: 0191 222 6000
Fax: 0161 222 6442

Wellness Forum
31 Great Peter Street
London SW1P 3LR
Tel: 0171 222 2332
Fax: 0171 222 2030

Wolfson Institute of Occupational Health
University of Dundee,
Level 5
Medical School
Ninewells
Dundee DD1 9SY
Tel: 01382 223181
Fax: 01382 644197

International Organisations

The Bureau of National Affairs Inc
1231 25th Street
NW Washington DC 20037
USA
Tel: +1 202 452 4200
Fax: +1 202 452 4084

Commission of European Communities
200 Rue de la Loi
B 1049 Brussels
Tel: +322 299 1111

European Foundation for the Improvemnet of Living & Working Conditions
Loughlinstown House
Shankill Co
Dublin
Ireland
Tel: +353 1204 3100

International Commission on Occupational Health
Department of Community
Occupational & Family Medicine
National University Hospital
Lower Kent Ridge Road
Singapore
Tel: +65 779 5555

International Institute of Risk & Safety Management
National Safety Centre
Chancellors Road
London W6 9RS
Tel: 0181 741 1231
Fax: 0181 741 4555

International Occupational Safety & Health Information Centre
154 Rue de Lausanne
CH 1211 Geneva 22
Switzerland
c/o International Labour Office
Vincent House
Vincent Square
London
Tel: 0171 828 6401
Fax: 0171 233 5925

Office of Disease Prevention & Health Promotion
Room 2132 Switzer Building
330 C Street
SW Washington DC 2021
USA
Tel: +1 404 639 3311

World Health Organisation
CH 1211 Geneva 27
Switzerland
Tel: +41 22 791 2111

Consultancy Services

AMI Health Care Group Plc
Corporate Health Services & Lifestyle Health Screening
4 Cornwall Terrace
Regents Park
London NW1 4QP
Tel: 0171 486 1266

Artus Associates
The Cedars
95 Crescent Road
Reading RG1 5SL
Tel: 0118 9508141
Fax: 01189 508101

BUPA Medical Centre
Webb House
210 Pentonvile Road
London N1 9TA
Tel: 0171 837 6484
Fax: 0171 837 6797

Cheviot Occupational Stress Management
Cheviot Consultancy Ltd
Heron House
5 Heron Square
Richmond
Surrey TW9 1EL
Tel: 0181 332 1842
Fax: 0181 332 2482

J & S Blenard Associates
Avril Cottage
48 Brockham Lane
Brockham
Betchworth
Surrey RH3 7EH
Tel: 01737 842256
Fax: 01737 842256

Norwich Union Risk Services
The Oaks
Clews Road
Oakenshaw
Redditch
Worcester B98 7ST
Tel: 01527 536 000
Fax: 01527 536 001

Otter Consultancy
8 Warwick Deeping
Ottershaw
Surrey KT18 0NE
Tel: 01932 873159
Fax: 01932 873159

PPP Preventitive Health Services
New Cavendish Medical Centre
99 New Cavendish Street
London W1M 7FQ
Tel: 0171 388 2468
Fax: 01892 515143

Sandwell Occupational Health
30 Hallam Close
Hallam Street
West Browich
West Midlands
Tel: 0121 607 3417
Fax: 0121 607 3420

Sedgwick Noble Lowndes Occupational Health Ltd
Washford House
Claybrook Drive
Redditch
Worcestershire B98 0DU
Tel: 01527 517747
Fax: 01527 525934

Sources: Health & Safety Executive, Merseyside and the British Medical Association, London

Index

NOTE: Italicized references indicate figures or tables.

Index of Advertisers